ENDURANCE RIDING

From First Steps to 100 Miles

ENDURANCE RIDING

From First Steps to 100 Miles

CLARE WILDE

KENILWORTH
PRESS

First published in Great Britain 1996 by
Kenilworth Press
Addington
Buckingham
MK18 2JR

British Library Cataloguing in Publication Data
A CIP record for this book is available from the British Library

ISBN 1-872082-83-1

Typeset in Optima and 10.5/13 Arrus
Design, typesetting and layout by Kenilworth Press
Printed and bound in Great Britain by
Hillman Printers (Frome) Ltd

*Frontispiece: The spirit of endurance riding, a sport that is truly accessible to
allcomers: horse and rider enjoying each other's company in beautiful countryside.*

Contents

Photo credits

Eric Jones: 14, 19, 21, 26, 33, 37, 40 *(both)*, 41, 42, 46, 53, 56, 57, 60, 72, 75, 82 *(top right & left)*, 86 *(left)*, 87, 89, 90, 92, 96, 98, 111, 113 *(left)*, 118, 120, 121, 127, 128, 129, 136, 137, 139, 143, 144, 148, 149, 152, 153, 154, 158, 160 *(left)*, 166, 170
Janet Harber: 35, 52, 71, 82 *(bottom)*, 86 *(right)*, 108, 113 *(right)*, 119, 132 *(both)*
Clare Wilde: 68, 103, 124, 133
Peter Orr: 45, 63
Gill Eyre: 24
John Birt: 160 *(right)*
David Osborne: *Frontispiece*

Acknowledgements

With sincere thanks to all those who have so freely given their time and assistance in the production of this book.

To Eric Jones, for his kindness, for always unfailingly producing the goods throughout the time I have known him, and for having an eye for a magical shot. To Theresa Hollands for her sound advice and her dedication to equine performance nutrition.

To Mark White, a seriously talented farrier who can be trusted to fix anything – the best it has been my pleasure to work with. To Ossie Hare, Stephen Humphreys, Wendy Dunham and all at the EHPS, and to Maggie and Claire at the ERG for their help and hard work.

To Janet Harber, Robbie Richardson, Joan Collins and all those who provided exactly what I needed for this book. To Thea Baker and Tony Ferrige, without whom I would not be where I am today. To Geoff and Angela Bloomfield, heartfelt thanks for your patience, generosity and support. To Keith Bryan for saddling my horses.

To Joyce Donnan, for breeding horses the like of which is rarely seen today. To Di Hey for knowing a match made in heaven. To Jan Benson, for having the vision and tenacity to give me the chance to found my own dynasty of Anglos, and continue in small part Joyce's work. To Josie Mills for opening the whole can of worms, and Fraise for teaching me to really ride.

To Richard, truly my better half, for believing in me. To all those competitors, friends, vets, ride organisers, helpers; my loyal, tolerant and professional crew, and all those who make the sport the wonderful pastime it is – without you, we'd have nothing.

To 'The Pioneers' – you know who you are! – for the inspiration that fuels the enthusiasm to keep us all going.

But most of all, to April Airs, the horse of a lifetime, who has given me the great privilege of knowing her and enjoying so many miles and moments together, and who has made so many dreams a reality.

Introduction

The horse has been used as a means of transport and recreation by man ever since we first encountered one another. Endurance riding has existed in one form or another, either as pleasure or from necessity, since that history began. However, this most fascinating and demanding aspect of man's partnership with horse has only been recognised as an organised equestrian discipline fairly recently.

A brief history

The founder of modern endurance riding was Wendell Robie, who organised the first ever Tevis Cup 100-miler in the US in 1955. It was from his inspiration and guidance that the sport blossomed worldwide and the US still leads the field in research, training, management techniques, innovation of equipment, endurance horse breeding and performance. The sport spread to the UK shortly afterwards with the first 50-mile Golden Horseshoe rides being run during the 1960s.

Through the enthusiasm and hard work of Ann Hyland, who came to the UK with her record-breaking homebred Arab stallion Nizzolan, the Endurance Horse and Pony Society was formed in 1973 as the UK's first official endurance riding organisation and governing body. This was closely followed in 1975 by the formation of the BHS Endurance Riding group (or Long Distance Riding Group as it was known then). It was in this year that the EHPS ran the first ever 100-miler in a day in the UK, the Summer Solstice ride. These original, early-established rides are still the most prestigious and sought-after titles in this country, with entries over 120 at the now 100-mile Golden Horseshoe in Exmoor every year, and competitors at the Solstice breaking national speed records almost annually.

The sport today

Today the BHS ERG sends teams of riders abroad every year, giving supervised experience of international competition to a Young Riders' team, an Intermediate and a Senior International squad, with strong representations and some resounding successes at the alternate annual European and World championships. Selection rides for the teams are held annually and riders spend many years in preparation for team-place listings.

A breakthrough for the UK came in 1993 when we hosted the European Championships for the first time, at Southwell racecourse in Nottinghamshire. As the sport is so young and still very much in its formative years, new administrative organisations and enthusiasts' clubs are constantly forming. The UK is also home to the Scottish Endurance Riding Club, formed during the 1980s and now a thriving and extremely active group, organising their own Scottish Championships 100-miler every year. More recently the embryonic Irish Long Distance Riding Association was set up, to initiate the growth and organisation of the sport in Ireland.

What endurance can offer you

Endurance riding is currently booming, with membership of the societies constantly on the increase. The ERG and EHPS now co-operate and work together more and more on various projects to raise the profile, popularity and accessibility of the sport. The abundance of trophies presented annually by each society provides recognition of riders' achievements from the 25-mile novice championship cup, under 14.2hhs awards, junior and veteran trophies, to the high-point senior mileage and race-riding awards.

Each body has an organised system of ride classification, aimed at education in every aspect of horse preparation and management through ride qualification. Qualifications begin with short distance rides of 20 and 25 miles, which must be completed to a set time, passing veterinary inspections pre- and post-ride. Riders at the top end of the spectrum progress right through to one-day 100-milers and multi-day 150-mile races. Each system is designed to attract newcomers and offer enjoyment and achievement at every step of the way. Even to the experienced and seasoned endurance rider, nothing provides more pleasure or sense of satisfaction than bringing out a novice, young horse and spending several seasons carefully producing him for top-level competition.

Who does endurance?

Endurance riding is probably the most accessible equine discipline today. Over the shortest distances, almost any horse and rider can achieve some measure of success, provided that horses are sound and adequately prepared. The sport embraces riders and horses of all ages, types and levels of ability. Riders come into endurance from every sphere, from showing or racing Arabs to hunting and carriage driving. Even at prestigious events nationally and internationally, cobs, warmbloods and even Haflingers compete alongside Arabs, Thoroughbreds and purpose-bred endurance horses. The feeling of success in completing your chosen distance, and being awarded merit purely on the strength of your horse's speed and finishing condition, make this an exciting and fulfilling discipline.

A challenge of your own

The motto of the sport worldwide is 'to complete is to win', and the personal and individual achievement that comes from challenging the terrain and the clock, rather than just other riders, makes every successful competitor a winner in his or her own right. Riders who are not competitive can concentrate on improving their own and their horse's performance at their chosen level. Those with big ambition go on to race and win the ultimate challenge of 100 miles in a day, and to compete internationally.

Once bitten by the distance bug, the craving for more miles, more demanding terrain and more breathtaking scenery sees riders specialising. Attention is turned towards breeding and buying horses for the job, and dedicating many years at a time to training and producing an equine athlete in the peak of physical fitness and condition.

Endurance as an education

By offering such a unique challenge, the sport also provides education in training and management; and at last, having been for many years treated by other disciplines as the poor cousin, other sports are coming to see the value of our methods and techniques.

The sport has developed as a demanding test of fitness for the very fittest, with the criteria throughout the stringent veterinary checks being to finish with a horse fit to continue. It also provides an ideal means of education for a young horse, and the relaxed and intuitive management and training that go into producing a young or novice endurance horse forms a partnership between man and horse that evolves like no other.

Veterinary control

Emphasis is on veterinary control at every step of the way – the endurance horse is probably the most carefully monitored equine athlete competing today. For newcomers to the sport, reassurance comes in the knowledge that rigorous veterinary checks ensure that any sign of stress is picked up before it becomes a problem. Later, races are won not just on riding speed but on fast 'vet-gate' presentation, so that management and preparation become more important than just riding at this level. Apart from winning, the most coveted and sought-after prize is the Best Condition award, given to the horse that the vets feel would be most fit to continue. In fact, receiving this award after a gruelling and difficult ride means more to many riders than actually winning the race.

The preparation and skill that go into producing a successful endurance horse have ensured that our sport has pioneered all kinds of management techniques, from monitoring and preventing dehydration to specialist feeding, temperature control and metabolic management; from new types of performance shoeing to innovative equipment design and original training methods.

A unique sport

Endurance riding has therefore become a unique sport, offering challenge and achievement to horses and riders from all walks of life, in some of the remotest corners of the world. The most successful long-term endurance partnerships are formed by riders spending many seasons in competition, training and producing carefully bred and selected horses to the absolute peak of fitness and physical condition. The successful endurance horse is an extraordinary athlete, at top levels covering 100 miles in record-breaking time over the most rugged and demanding terrain known to man, then trotting out the next day for Best Condition judging, as fresh and relaxed as if it had spent the week in a field. The dedication, commitment and determination involved in endurance riding are second to none and, what to many riders appears an improbable achievement, becomes possible entirely through individual preparation and hard work.

Having said all of this, endurance riding is also enormous fun, the key words being preparation and observation. All comers can achieve some measure of success, and because of that endurance riding very quickly becomes a dedicated, exclusive and professional way of life. The emphasis should always be on enjoying yourself and your horse, and the company of other riders, with whom a lasting bond of friendship is formed over many miles spent together. This sport combines the ultimate challenge with enormous educational value, and the best excuse in the world to spend hours in the company of a beautiful horse and the people you like most, in remote and peaceful parts of the country.

In this book, we will be looking at every aspect of endurance riding, from assessing and choosing a horse, to racing 100 miles. The aim is to provide a comprehensive guide to the sport for riders at every level, imparting essential information to complete newcomers, and suggesting tips and advice for success and enjoyment at any distance.

1

Selecting a Horse

Endurance riding demands that a horse is able to pass stringent veterinary checks during competition. When selecting a horse for this type of work, you need to look for the animal that will be best able to complete the distance in good shape. If you hope to ride competitively, you need a horse that will complete the distance faster and in better shape than the other horses. If you were choosing a car for long-distance rallying, you would go for one that was most economical on petrol, oil and parts – reducing the likelihood of it breaking down, overheating or running into other problems en route. You'd also look for a car that could cruise comfortably but that, if you put your foot down, could produce a good turn of speed too. These same principles apply when you are looking for a horse for endurance riding.

The truth behind the myth

There are certain attributes which will make a horse more likely to work with a low pulse rate, recover quickly, and suffer the minimum physical stress and attrition (wear and tear). Certain types of horse often seem to do well and, on further analysis, they are shown to possess a number of attributes which give them an advantage over the rest of the field. Animals possessing all those attributes obviously have the best chance of making it to the top. In this chapter we will consider not only what is necessary for a successful competition horse, but what might give your own animal that winning edge.

While horses with old injuries, conformational weaknesses and odd action do compete, such problems place them at an unfair disadvantage. The stress to which they are subjected is increased, making them more likely to sustain injuries and to tire more quickly than horses without problems. Generally speaking, this will limit the level at which these horses can compete, either in regard to the distance which they can complete comfortably or the speed at which they can work with ease.

In order to prevent problems occurring with your own mount, it is

An ideal endurance horse: excellent limbs, well-shaped feet and super conformation and attitude.

important to take everything steadily and never to place unfair demands on him. Therefore, you need to assess carefully your own animal's strengths and weaknesses and set realistic targets to achieve. That way, when you reach your own particular horse's limits, common sense should tell you that this is as far, or as fast, as you can reasonably go. Years ago, some unlikely horses became champions, and today, due to greater knowledge and modern preparation and feeding techniques, many horses can comfortably complete 100 miles at a steady pace. However, to win at top international level at today's speeds, a supreme athlete is required, and not every horse is able to meet the criteria. So when considering what it takes to make an athlete and what to look for in your potential endurance horse, remember that in reality, perfection is just a myth and we have to make the best of the available material.

The basics

You are primarily looking for an economical, durable animal who will produce consistently low pulse rates and stay sound during a long period of work. As you will know yourself if you exercise regularly, physical work for a sustained length of time produces heat as a by-product of muscular and metabolic activity. All that heat needs to be dispersed, to prevent the body from overheating. A hot body employs a number of methods to try and dissipate heat, such as panting and sweating. To keep metabolic rates down, therefore, it is of fundamental importance to keep an endurance horse cool. A cool horse is far more likely to return a low pulse rate during vetting (unless something else is wrong). If he is hot, he will be panting, sweating, and his heart will be pumping away to fuel all the activity.

Heat dissipation

So to throw off the heat that is generated internally, you want a horse that is built to self-cool and dissipate his own heat as far as possible. A really deep girth, flat sides and a fairly narrow body all help to radiate the heat within. Internal heat has a shorter distance to go to reach the outside; air cooling takes places as the wind passes over the horse's flat sides, and water can be sloshed over them with ease. Barrel-shaped horses are not only more difficult to cool down from a crew's point of view, but from their own; the greater proportion of their surface areas are not best placed to receive the breeze. A surface area that is larger underneath is facing towards the ground, which may also be hot; core heat is farther away from the outside of the horse and harder to disperse.

Size and pulse rate

While basic conformation may have a bearing upon certain horse's ability to throw off heat and maintain a steady temperature, heart rates may also be reliant upon other inherited or genetic factors. There is a lot of talk about horses with 'big hearts' that pump a greater volume of blood, working more efficiently and at a lower pulse rate than other horses. Veterinary opinion varies as to whether or not this theory is supported by tangible evidence, but there are certainly horses on the circuit who seem to work within almost unnaturally low parameters. How much this has to do with the horse's basic fitness and preparation, as well as other factors like individual temperament and natural excitability, has yet to be determined.

Pulse parameters have certainly improved during the recent years – though, again, this may be due to more rigorous preparation or in-depth management knowledge than in earlier years. Small horses and ponies will always return higher rates than bigger horses, just as a mouse has a faster heart rate than an elephant. Any question over the optimum size for an endurance horse therefore has to take into account metabolic parameters, body shape, body mass or weight and stride length, as well as speed and economy of management. Bulky or very big horses tend not to be fast or manoeuvrable and may have problems keeping cool if they have a high body weight and volume. From observation, and without conducting a survey, the commonest height for horses on the circuit tends to be between 15hh and 15.3hh. This is obviously dependent on rider requirements and preference; there are plenty of 14.2hh and 16.2hh animals doing extremely well, each with their own talents and special qualities.

Feet

An endurance horse's feet have to cope with plenty of wear and tear over the miles, both in training and during competition. Because of the mileage involved, they also tend to be shod far more frequently than horses in other disciplines. These two factors combined necessitate a really superb set of feet. Look for a good hoof size in relation to the horse's body: too tiny, and they won't absorb much shock or bear much weight; too large, and the feet get heavy and tiring for the horse to move during sustained work. Very flat soles are more prone to bruising than concave soles, which can lead to real problems over much of the difficult terrain where endurance rides are held.

A good 50-55° hoof-pastern axis is also essential. Too low a heel can place all kinds of strain on the leg, as well as the foot itself, and may be a factor in the development of navicular. Too high a heel allows for little movement in the axis and little absorption of concussion. Pasterns should be well formed and not too short or long – they are going to have to absorb plenty of shock during the horse's career. Although Arabs tend to be the most frequently used breed for the sport, their feet are rarely perfect and may tend towards being small, boxy and upright. An open heel is essential, to help absorb shock as efficiently as possible. A good, dense quality of horn is obviously going to suffer the least wear and tear and hold shoes on better than weaker, more porous horn. Weak hoof horn characteristically looks flaky or cracked. However, there is a great deal that can be done, largely through dietary management, to improve poor horn quality.

Stride and action

All of these ingredients begin to add up to a basic skeletal formation to look for in an endurance horse. The way a horse is put together also has a fundamental influence on stride length. In order to use the least energy, travel with the minimum possible effort and cover the largest piece of ground with each step, a horse with a long, low stride is preferable. Look for a well-angled, sloping shoulder, a well set-on, correctly made neck and, above anything else, the straight flight of the limb. If a horse moves from his shoulder naturally, he will cover the ground well. Conformation allowing, some horses need to be taught to stride out and are simply in the habit of pottering about. As with any horse, the animal's basic way of going can often be vastly improved through schooling and training.

Most people will just trot a horse away from you to show that he is sound when you are buying him, which allows little opportunity for a real examination of the animal's action. When looking at a prospective endurance horse, always watch him trot out from the side, to gauge how free a stride he has and whether he tracks up properly. Watch him trot out from behind and in front too, to see if his legs move straight and freely and that he is level. Any odd stride characteristics may be due to, or indicative of problems elsewhere and simply mean extra work for the horse.

A horse that brushes is far more likely to injure himself when tired; and dishing or plaiting require more effort from the horse to move each limb – again, when the animal becomes too tired to move his legs out of his own way after a long day over hard terrain, you may have trouble. A naturally well-balanced stride is a bonus, but again, balance can be improved with schooling. Having said all this, don't look for perfection. It is truly rare to find the exceptionally good paces that many people believe their horses have – but you won't be in any doubt if you come across a real mover! There are few horses who can't be taught, with a little schooling and correct muscling up, to work more economically. It is worth a reminder that the limb itself should meet all the requirements of generally good conformation: a fair amount of flat, dense bone; good joints, well let-down hocks and knees, short cannons that are set on straight, and so on.

Head, neck and wither

Balance of the whole horse and stride length is also largely related to the conformation of the neck and head. A horse with a very long neck or large head will have to devote more energy to holding his head up. This sort of conformation also tends to bring the basic centre of balance forward and encourage the horse to travel on his forehand. Similarly, a very short or thick neck tends to go with a horse that pulls himself along from the front and may have a fairly short stride. A very chunky neck may not allow enough freedom of the gullet and windpipe, but a clearly defined windpipe and large nostrils help to accommodate the vast amounts of oxygen that a horse uses during fast or sustained work.

It is preferable to have a good wither which will hold the saddle in place over every kind of terrain; frequently, a good wither comes with a good shoulder.

Hindquarters

As with any horse, the endurance horse's basic power should come from behind. He is going to have to propel himself across all sorts of country-side and he needs to get up and down hills with the least possible effort. For a horse to be able to bring his back end underneath and move in a balanced way, good loins and quarters are vital. A strong, well-made back end is therefore the ideal; but this does not mean quarters with big muscles. A horse with big, round or bunchy, shortened muscles is harder to keep cool as he will tend to hold the heat. To encourage heat-loss and minimise bulk, look for flat, lean muscles.

Body shape

The overall picture, then, is that of a streamlined, lightweight but tough athlete; a strong but light frame, well muscled but not bulky – the marathon runner of the equine world. To the unpractised eye, endurance horses may look underweight – but so do marathon runners! This look is purely due to the lack of excess baggage being carried, in the form of fat. Basic body shape, if you were to look from the top, should be flat sided, or slightly wedge-shaped. A horse with a well-sprung rib cage will have more room for his lungs to expand and take in oxygen, as well as keeping his saddle in place. Though it may be a lightweight, a very shallow horse with a round barrel is not at an advantage here.

Skin

Skin should be thin but tough, with the veins visibly close to the surface for extra-efficient heat dissipation and easy cooling. Skin pigment is also worth a serious look – curiously enough, pink skin sometimes appears to be weaker than blue or grey skin. There appears to be no proven scientific reason why this should occur, but pink skin (or skin without pigment) anywhere on the horse's body can be more vulnerable to damage. The main area to look out for is around the feet, as pink heels seem more prone to bacterial infection and cracking, which can cause unsoundness and general discomfort, though this is not always the rule. Such cracking can actually occur during a high mileage ride and is exacerbated by washing to cool a horse down, or working through wet, boggy ground. It is also said that darker-coloured horses may suffer more stress in hot climates, though in the UK this problem isn't generally a consideration. Heat stress may become a relevant issue, however, if competing abroad is an option. Body hair must also be considered as, though endurance horses working at high mileages are often clipped out even during the summer, a hairy horse will retain more heat and suffer more stress than one with a lighter smattering of coat.

Temperament

The temperament and psychological profile of an athletic horse has plenty of bearing on both the selection of a specialist horse and the assessment of your own. 'Difficult' horses are sometimes put into endurance work because the long hours at a steady speed tend to encourage them to relax. Uptight horses are often mistaken for being energetic, but may well be running purely on nervous excitement and tire just as quickly as a more relaxed individual. A very fit, well-fed 'difficult' animal is not the easiest candidate to take into demanding or strange situations on a regular basis, or to stable away from home, without suffering more stress than is entirely necessary for both the horse and his

Khairho, a consistent endurance race performer. Well put together and a super outlook.

handlers. Animals with flighty, easily excited or upset natures tend to produce erratic heart rates, which can be very difficult to manage during competition, as well as being problematical for ride vets to cope with.

Ideally, you should look for a laid-back, relaxed and confident horse that you feel happy about taking anywhere and doing anything with. Bravery and honesty in the horse are essential. If your horse is prepared to try when you ask him to try, you can hope for nothing more. An endurance horse may have to work alone for many long hours, go first, last or in a pack, or jockey for position during a mass start. These horses become used to co-operating as a matter of course, as well as using their initiative. They need to really enjoy working – it's impossible to bully a horse into winning! There is a recognisable 'extra something' that can help both horse and rider overcome some difficult situations, and encourage the flagging horse to produce a racing finish, then calm down again for a vetting afterwards.

Of the utmost importance, though, is that the two of you get on. Bearing in mind the amount of time that you are likely to spend in your horse's company, if your personalities clash, it's just not going to work. It is true to a certain extent that a calm rider produces a calm horse; however, if you are both generally grumpy or highly strung, sparks will fly!

Breeding

Anyone will tell you that Arabs are predominantly used for endurance work: they are said to be more suited to it than any other breed. Over the years, various surveys and studies have been carried out in an attempt to determine whether Arabs actually perform better than other horses. Whether they do, or whether it just looks as though they do because there are so many more on the circuit than any other breed, is still a matter of some debate. However, with the advent of cheaper imports, breeds native to other countries and purpose-bred endurance horses, there is plenty to choose from other than the typical pure-bred Arab. It is worth bearing in mind that not every type or strain of Arab has the most ideal conformation for the sport.

Plenty of people will tell you that unless you have an Arab, you won't succeed – which, of course, is simply not true. There is an increasing amount of other blood being used and there are plenty of ideas about what breed the 'endurance horse' should be. Part-bred Arabs, including some Thoroughbred and native blood, or Anglo-Arabs, with their extra size, quality and scope are increasingly popular today, as well as unusual breeds and unregistered horses. Once you have found your own particular 'ideal', it is easy to develop tunnel vision and not look objectively at the merits of other breeds. With any horse, bloodlines are worth taking into account, as there are lines of Thoroughbreds, Arabs, Morgans and others which have consistently performed well in virtually every sphere.

The endurance horse

Throughout long years of competition, there have been some horses who have gone on and on, mile after mile, seemingly for ever. These typical little toughies are often of unknown or unregistered breeding, but have exactly what it takes to succeed in this demanding sport. They have light frames but are unremarkable to look at, except that they have the vital ingredients for endurance, often proving to be very fast with it. How much this has to do with their breeding and how much their management is indeterminable. Arab/Thoroughbred/Native crosses are the preferred combination, in a ratio of about 50% Arab, 25% Thoroughbred and 25% Native blood. Today, purpose-bred endurance horses are being produced by competitors from ex-endurance horses that have been consistently successful. These include part-bred Morgans and part-bred Arabs, as well as pure-bred Arabs and some Appaloosa crosses. All tend to have a dash of Thoroughbred, a typically light but strong frame, a sensible outlook and tough appearance. Several offspring of former champion endurance horses are now competing and proving to be extremely successful.

An Arab is not the only endurance horse! A well prepared coloured cob covering the ground at speed.

Arabs and part-breds

The pure-bred Arab is the favourite of many for endurance work as it has plenty of enduring qualities: tough little feet, thin skin, a long stride, an intelligent nature, gentle temperament and big nostrils to take in lots of air. They are gutsy, determined and committed characters, who will perform to the boundaries of their ability if handled and produced well. They require a fairly devoted owner as they absolutely adore company and, in the right hands, prove to be loyal, outstandingly talented athletes. They are nippy, fast and tough and have strong little backs which, if very close-coupled, can be difficult to fit for saddles. However, there is currently a glut of Arabs being bred commercially and the quality of some stock is decidedly dubious; offset cannons are a common problem as is a lack of bone, weak legs, sky-high hocks, a shallow barrel and badly made quarters. Their foot conformation may tend to predispose them to concussive problems. In the wrong hands, they can also develop behavioural problems, as they are sensitive, easily offended and have long memories.

Part-bred Arabs, with a dash of Native, are often tougher and more serviceable than a pure-bred and can be easier to manage. The most typical combination is a dash of Connemara or Welsh blood, resulting in some stunning animals of amazing stamina and strength. Though they tend to be fairly small, the speed that these little horses produce is incredible, and their determination has to be seen to be believed. They are easy to get fit as they adore working, and consistently do their utmost to please. Their feet may have better basic construction than a pure-bred. However, there is a peculiarly hot temperament that can accompany an Arab/Welsh cross, with a certain panic-point triggered occasionally by stress.

Thoroughbreds and Anglo-Arabs

Thoroughbreds are bigger, scopier and have longer, more ground-covering paces than Arabs. Their feet, however, tend to flatness and they may come with high withers. Their straight hind limb conformation is also rarely ideal for propelling a rider and tack up and down steep hills. My own personal favourite is the Anglo-Arab or Arab/Thoroughbred cross, as the extra size and scope makes for a horse that sails along at an easy, relaxed trot, when all around are bundling along behind at a canter.

Slightly bigger horses often manage difficult terrain more easily, especially over places like Exmoor where there is very boggy or deep terrain, or very rocky ground. Their feet can provide the ideal compromise, with excellent concave soles. If well bred and intelligently handled, they gather the best qualities of the Arab and Thoroughbred, in terms of both conformation and character. They have wonderfully calm, laid-back temperaments and thrive on work, challenge, and the hours of human attention that go with endurance riding. Their inherent stamina allows even the average Anglo to go on for ever. They do, however, need sensitive handling due to the alert mentality that accompanies any amount of Thoroughbred blood. These horses are naturally extremely gentle and loyal and, if hurt or upset, they never, ever forget. Any handler must always think well ahead and have some insight into the equine mentality, as an Anglo will happily work flat out until it drops. The combination a good Anglo with an owner committed to working with and listening to the animal, forms an outstanding partnership in terms of performance, mutual respect and affection.

Appaloosas

Appaloosas are becoming ever more popular and often have an in-bred toughness and determination which is hard to find elsewhere. The best of these horses are ideally built for travelling and have a natural, long-striding trot that goes on and on. Their feet are notoriously well formed of dense, hard horn. Crossing with other breeds is producing some really nice horses of a very athletic type, but beware of those that are too heavy or have very bunchy muscles. In the USA there is a passion for the Arab/Appaloosa cross, which is equivalent to the Arab/Thoroughbred/Native type. These horses have the wonderful paces of the two breeds combined, and really look the part. This particular cross produces some horses of remarkably gentle nature which, backed by athletic ability, provides the raw ingredients for a top endurance horse.

Trakehner crosses

Trakehner crosses are worth a close look. When crossed with lighter Thoroughbreds or Arabs, they produce some outstanding quality and very tough, extremely fast horses – several almost unbeatable champions have had half Trakehner blood. They tend to have excellent, beautifully balanced paces, and are also extremely work-minded, happily concentrating on the task in hand to the exclusion of more minor distractions which would upset a flightier horse. The extra strength and quality of the Trakehner quarters provide a real powerhouse of a motor, keeping this type of horse cruising at top speed when all around are failing.

Morgans

Morgans are becoming increasingly popular, either in pure- or part-bred form. There are at least two breeders of endurance horses in the UK and elsewhere who tend to concentrate on part-bred Morgans and, as

Triella (Willow), a supremely successful endurance mare, by an Arab stallion out of a Welsh/TB mare. Willow is a Grade 1 HIS mare, shown here with her fourth foal, Trioletta, by the HIS stallion Rubicund. Willow's other three foals are all in endurance homes.

imports are now more affordable and accessible, this is another breed well worth considering. Their feet and legs are generally very well constructed and ideally suited to long hours of hard work. In the US they have long been recognised for their stamina and affability, achieving some incredible endurance performances. Due to their versatility they frequently make all-round top-class athletes, providing their owners with a lifetime's achievement and loyalty.

Russian breeds

The variety of Russian breeds being brought into the country should produce some interesting careers during the next few years. As yet there are few on the circuit, but some are showing real promise. Tersk horses, particularly, are being used as a larger, rangier and tougher alternative to the Arab, with the speed to match. Tersks are also being produced, both pure- and part-bred, as endurance horses. Other Russian breeds are now available on import and there has been a great deal of interest, particularly in the Akhal-Teke. It is thought that the rugged desert existence in their native habitats should predispose these horses to endurance work and, in their own countries, this certainly seems to be true.

Trotters, Quarter horses and Standardbreds

Pacers and trotting types have regularly done well over recent years. They tend to be naturally tough, hardy and largely unflappable, with an incredible turn of speed. There are only a few on the circuit but as they are affordable, and so far unspoilt by the whims of commercial breeding in this country, they are worth closer consideration. There are also numerous American breeds such as Quarter horses and Standardbreds quietly but successfully competing. These deserve promotion and recognition by the endurance riding fraternity and a closer look by any prospective purchaser.

Ponies

Natives and native crosses can often prove more difficult to produce for endurance work, as they are naturally bulky and quite heavily muscled. In pure form, breeds such as Fells, Connemaras and Welsh Cobs and ponies, are worth considering if you are looking for a tough, serviceable little horse to compete consistently at a steady speed. During recent years there has been at least one successful Haflinger at international level. Even Icelandic horses are being used and it is claimed that their weight-carrying ability is unsurpassed, though they have yet to appear in top-level competition.

Where to look

The vast majority of riders begin by competing with the horse they already own. This is undoubtedly the best way to start out in the sport, and you will learn enough to show a younger or more novice horse the ropes, should you decide to make a special buy in the future. You may even have a potential champion sitting in your stable – alternatively, you may have to be happy with settling at a certain level of work. Almost any horse should be able to complete 20 miles, and many will surprise their owners with their propensity for distance work. It is always worth carefully and objectively assessing your horse's strengths and weaknesses before you start any training and fitness programme.

If you decide to make a special purchase, take your time. There is no point in rushing out to buy an endurance horse, as you are extremely unlikely to find the perfect potential athlete in the first place you look. The right horse is notoriously hard to track down; plenty of people buy an excellent youngster and just wait. There are those who breed endurance horses specifically for the job, and these are the first people to contact if you want a really good youngster at a realistic price. There are also plenty of superb horses that come out of race training, be they Arabs, Anglos or Thoroughbreds. The obvious main advantage with a

A good sort for endurance. All the right ingredients in a tough little frame and a hardy outlook.

horse that is used to competing is that he will be accustomed to travelling and going to new places.

Buying a horse straight off the stud is not always a good idea, as very in-bred horses can have conformational and temperamental problems. Many commercial breeders have so much youngstock that none is given the necessary basic handling, which results in a stroppy, undisciplined youngster. Nothing can make up for good basic training. A horse that has been left to get on with life for three years is unlikely to become as tractable as the youngster who has been carefully handled, right from the start. On the other hand, lots of youngsters bred to show have excellent conformation which, as we have established, is the basis for a horse that can really perform.

2

Feet and Shoeing

The sheer mileage involved in endurance riding tests a horse's feet and shoes to a greater extent than any other equine sport. The preparation to get a horse fit for endurance involves plenty of mileage during training at home, before even embarking on a ride. Add to this a full season of fixtures, and it is easy to see how training and competitive miles combine to wear shoes out fast, no matter what the terrain. As it is advisable to take a horse to a competitive ride recently shod, you will need a visit from the farrier at least every four weeks under normal circumstances during the season. In some cases shoes wear out far more quickly than this, for example during a mountainous or very hard ride, or where lots of work on hard tracks and roads is involved.

The potential effects of the concussion from all this work are enormous, as is the attrition to be sustained from working hard over all types of ground. In order to be able to perform consistently well in spite of this, your horse's feet have to be kept in premium condition. Well-kept hoof horn increases the chances of shoes staying on, and gives a head start on wear and tear. To help to keep horn in good condition, feet should ideally sustain minimal damage from the work itself. Shoes should therefore be designed to protect the foot, be durable and long-lasting, and to take as much of the strain as possible. Endurance shoeing attempts to encompass all of these requirements. During this chapter we will examine what to look for in a durable foot, what can be done to improve horn quality and how endurance shoeing strategy should be approached.

Basic foot conformation

An excellent foot is obviously the best starting point. The basic conformation of a durable foot should start with a correct hoof-pastern axis (approximately 50-55°). If the hoof-pastern axis is upright, flat or broken, this needs to be corrected before embarking on any serious training programme with your horse. An upright foot will not allow for much shock absorption and this in itself will encourage concussive problems. A very boxy foot may also be the result of navicular, so if in doubt, steer clear. A shallow axis and a foot that is flat on the ground place additional strain on the tendons, resulting in all kinds of detrimental conditions. This kind of conformation predisposes a horse to navicular.

Heels should be open and healthy, not collapsed or virtually non-existent. Shoeing with support at the heel is essential to any horse covering the amount of ground that an endurance horse does.

A healthy, rubbery frog is amongst the other fundamentally desirable qualities of an endurance foot, as is a substantial hoof wall. Thin hoof walls are prone to being brittle and may not afford enough of a foot to nail the shoe onto. A slightly concave sole, held a little farther off the ground than in a flat foot, will help to avoid stone bruising. The horn of the sole should be fairly thick, as thin soles are more susceptible to injury. Really dense horn has the best shock absorbency and is most likely to keep shoes on.

A good hoof size in relation to the horse's bodyweight is necessary to carry the horse's weight and your own over many miles, but it does not want to be too big – very large feet tend to be heavy, apart from generally coming with a very big horse, who would probably not be an ideal endurance candidate! Remember also that tiny equine feet have a similar effect to a human wearing a stiletto-heeled shoe. Weight concentrated through a small surface area will increase the strain to which the structures of the foot and the limb are subjected.

Foot balance

The balance of the foot and the way it is set on to the limb is something that, with a practised eye, you will also learn to examine. One of the most important points to note about the endurance horse's foot is that it should strike the floor in a balanced way. The foot should not roll to the inside or outside nor twist during a stride, as all of these actions place undue stress on the leg.

As you hold up the horse's foot, examine the hoof itself and look for a balanced basic shape, with no shearing or winging. Make sure that the pastern enters at the centre of the foot. Problems like these, and imbalances that show up as rolling, may have been caused by poor farriery, or might be purely conformational defects. Often they can be corrected again by skilful work, but may have caused foot and limb stresses in the meantime. A horse whose feet have severe conformational defects is unlikely to remain sound in hard work.

Action

Any odd or unbalanced movement wears the shoes unevenly. Therefore,

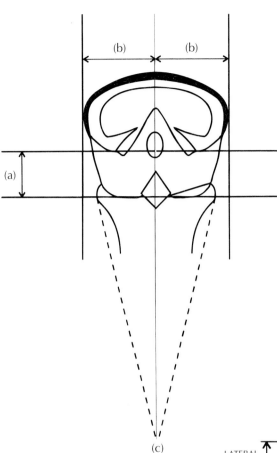

(c)

This is a position in which you will often see the foot and it is a good angle from which to assess balance.

• Are the heels the same length? (a)
• Is the distance from the centre of the frog to the outside of the foot the same on both sides? (b) (Especially in the hind feet!)
• Is the angle of the wall each side of the foot the same? In other words, if you were to draw a line up each side of the foot, would they meet in the centre of the leg? (c), also referred to here as Balance Point 1 (BP1).

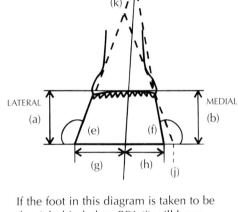

Viewing the foot from the front while it is on the ground: in this position you can also look for relevant angles and references. (a) and (b) should be the same; (g) and (h) should be the same; angles (e) and (f) should be the same. If a line were drawn up from each side of the foot it should meet in the centre on the leg at reference point (i) (BP1).

If the foot in this diagram is taken to be the right hind, then BP1 (i) will be on the inside. This will lead to strain on the outside of the leg, and in the case of the fetlock, can result in windgalls. The way to balance the foot is first to make sure that (g) and (h) are the same width, even if this means extending the shoe on the inside (j), for although the inside heel may be high, the lateral and the medial wall could be the same length. This means that angle (f) is too upright. By taking this action the BP1 (k) will move to the centre, thus starting the balancing process. The height of BP1 will differ from breed to breed. The more upright the foot the higher the BP1 will be.

Assessing foot balance. (Diagrams taken from 'The Horse's Foot and Related Problems' by R.C. Richardson.)

any spots where the shoes are unevenly worn or are exceptionally thin are worth further examination. The likelihood is that extra pressure is being directed through the worn place, via uneven weight distribution or through basic foot imbalance. Alternatively, there may be a twist coming from higher up the limb. Though shoe distress provides a good indication of where to look for the problem, were this horse to compete over any distance, such uneven wear could cause all sorts of problems. Any consistently stressful movement will limit the work that each particular horse can do.

All of the above problems are influenced by basic conformation and worth careful consideration before you buy a horse, or set targets for work. If your horse is very pigeon-toed, for example, the flight and movement of each limb will be influenced. A horse who dumps his toes will wear out his shoes in an inordinately short period of time, and undoubtedly will have problems higher up in his limbs. Additional stress sustained through the foot, and the corresponding reduction in shock absorption, will be transmitted to the leg, increasing the risk of injury through concussion or general stress and strain. There are horses with far less than perfect limbs whose feet, however, are set on straight and strike the floor correctly. If the foot is balanced, the limbs have a greater chance of remaining sound.

Horn quality

Following examination of conformation of the foot, horn quality is the next major consideration before a horse is even shod for endurance training. Basic hoof maintenance involves the same primary skills as all other areas of horse management: observation, assessment and action. Observe and assess your horse's horn quality on a regular basis and, if it is less than ideal, take action to improve it. Poor hoof horn will not stand much of a chance of holding a shoe on, and is more likely to sustain injury.

Horn quality can actually be transformed through good management techniques and careful dietary considerations. Today, there are many modern feed supplements which can top up various vitamin and mineral deficiencies. These tend to contain biotin, methionine and calcium (in the form of limestone flour) in various proportions and help to provide a new, stronger and denser quality of hoof growth. These supplements can also sufficiently increase the rate of horn growth to provide new horn upon which to fix each successive set of shoes. Sole growth and regrowth should also improve through feeding dietary supplements. Very thin soles thicken and become more springy, more dense, better able to withstand wear and repel bruising from stones.

However, the addition of any such supplement to the diet may serve to camouflage a basic dietary imbalance. Be sure that your horse's basic ration is nutritionally balanced before adding anything extra for a specific problem.

Moisture content

A constant moisture content in the hoof is vitally important to sustain good horn quality. Overly dry feet become brittle, due to loss of moisture from the cells. This can also occur in feet where the moisture content is constantly fluctuating, becoming soaked and then drying out again. The horn cracks and flakes, becoming progressively more prone to damage and unlikely to hold shoes on. Good stable management is essential to prevent feet from suffering the ill-effects of ammonia from the horse's urine and, though the weather cannot be controlled, moisture content in the hoof can be regulated to a certain degree.

Through the use of various preparations formulated to be applied to the outside of the hoof and sole, moisture content can be stabilised whilst allowing the foot to breathe. Where horn quality is very poor, these preparations can provide a substantial improvement in quality and strength. I don't know many horse owners, let alone farriers, who still recommend the use of hoof oils, which effectively seal the hoof. Modern preparations afford breatheability and exchange of moisture, protecting without completely sealing.

Of course, attention to the feet is an ongoing task and is part of the endurance horse's everyday management regime. Ideally any major attention should be carried out prior to the start of competitive work and a strong, dense hoof should be correctly prepared and shod to start the season.

Your farrier

Whilst no two feet, let alone no two sets of feet, are identical, the optimum set of feet for each individual can be achieved through good management and farriery. Generally speaking, very few horses have ideal foot shape or horn quality. Whilst basic foot conformation is established, an enormous amount can be done to improve what you first see, through skilled and thoughtful farriery. It is worth saying a word or two here about your farrier. Without a really good craftsman, your horse is unlikely ever to enjoy really good feet. If you are lucky enough to find a farrier who enjoys his work and takes a pride and an interest in each horse he does, treat him with the respect he deserves. Even with the escalating cost of shoeing today, it is worth paying more for a farrier who will travel further, or to box your horse to find the right person.

When you start out, ask other people at rides who they use, and find out where the ride farrier comes from, as he is likely to be the organiser's own. A skilful, attentive farrier can not only drastically improve the quality and shape of a horse's feet, but keep a horse going throughout a strenuous season. Finding something to nail the shoes onto can sometimes be a puzzle, but if your farrier can consistently shoe well and provide the best opportunity for those shoes staying on, your horse has a fighting chance of staying sound throughout the year. A farrier who is willing to pop in as he is passing to re-weld toes or tighten up clenches when necessary is a truly rare commodity and to be cherished. 'Best Shod Horse' and farriers' awards are given at numerous rides throughout the year and it is a real accolade to win one, bearing in mind the excellent standard of endurance shoeing in general. My own farrier is thrilled when he wins an award; it's not the nature of the prize, but he prides himself on the fact that he has done a better job than a hundred or so other farriers from all over the country.

Poor farriery

Poor shoeing, on the other hand, detrimentally affects the horse's way of going and will shorten his working life. There are too many horses in ordinary, non-competitive work that are shod to a low standard, with long toes and low heels. This in itself has, over the years, proved to be a recipe for disaster for any horse, let alone an endurance horse. Flat, shallow feet, continuously shod with long toes and low heels, encourage flexor tendon strain and contraction of the heels. The long-term result will be boxy growth and an increased chance of sustaining navicular. Though a great deal can be done to improve the soundness of a horse with navicular, he is unlikely ever to stay sound in very hard work for any length of time.

Corns can be caused through poor, over-tight shoeing, particularly at the heel. All kinds of other trouble can occur as a result of incorrect shoe placement, poor shoe shaping or inexact foot trimming, so it is worth waiting to find a good farrier rather than risk your horse's feet!

The endurance shoe

One of the major aims of any shoe is to protect the horse's foot, and correct basic shoeing is vital before any specialist shoe 'customising' is even considered. To protect and support as much of the wall and base of the foot as possible, wide-webbed shoes are often used on endurance horses. Endurance shoes should be built to last, for grip and to aid shock absorption, which is why a wide web is additionally favoured. The increased surface area provides added grip and wear, and is also said to aid shock absorption. The additional weight-bearing surface of wide-webbed shoes can be useful in therapeutic treatment of brittle feet.

Shoes of this design are also easier to shape with a rolled toe, which

On the left a standard shoe; on the right a wide-webbed shoe, more commonly used for endurance.

helps to prevent wear of the tip. A rolled toe shoe is often used to encourage an earlier breakover of the foot, staving off the occurrence of tripping and stumbling over difficult terrain or when your horse tires. Rolled toe shoes, however, unless custom made, have no toe clips, which do help to keep a shoe in place. Welded (borium) toes improve the life of shoes immensely and, if roughened, improve the grip. Strategically placed tungsten-cored nails will do the same job, and are particularly used to aid grip in the back corners. However, bear in mind that any added traction with the ground surface will correspondingly limit the slide factor of the shoe, particularly on the road. This may increase the stress to which the limbs are subjected. Tungsten nails should always be used in preference to studs as, over the course of the shoe's wear, they will create less of an imbalance in the foot than even the smallest pony stud.

Innovations

In view of the benefits, wide-webbed steel shoes are currently the most commonly seen endurance shoes. However, other types of shoe are regularly found, and ordinary horseshoes are more or less obsolete for this type of work. Endurance riders are notoriously willing to try anything that looks likely to improve on existing equipment. As modern materials, research and manufacturing techniques improve, a whole new generation of horseshoes are being produced, which can only be good news for endurance horses. Today, plenty of horses are competing with lightweight plastic shoes, rubber-coated steel shoes and alloy/plastic combinations. I know many riders who use these types of shoe and swear by them. The modern materials weigh only a tiny fraction of the weight of steel and, apart from providing an improved grip, they absorb many times more shock than steel, which helps to alleviate the effects of concussion. Because they weigh far less, horn quality improves and stride length and action can be considerably enhanced.

Some riders work their horses in ordinary wide-webbed steel shoes and have plastic, rubber or alloy shoes put on just before a ride, much as flat-racing horses working in aluminium plates do. The weight difference is said to reduce the fatigue to which the horse is subject and, apart from an increase in stride length, their use has been reported to effect beneficially the speed which can be sustained for any length of time. As with every benefit, there is a hidden drawback, and most alternative shoes are somewhat more costly than steel. Their life may also be slightly shorter; some riders overcome this by having tungsten nails put into the corners, though this will reduce the shock-absorbing properties of polyurethane shoes. Rubber-coated shoes, however, actually last longer than steel ones, providing better value for money.

Corrective work

Corrective shoeing and farriery can be extremely useful in amending the flight of the foot for balance and angle of placement. Heels of shoes should always be carefully bevelled and fitted. Just the right amount of shoe is necessary to protect and support the heels; any edges should always be carefully bevelled to prevent the risk of their wearing into sharp edges and slicing into the horse should he strike himself. Overly long heels in front may increase the chances of a shoe being trodden on and pulled off during work, particularly in deep going. This may occur if your horse is prone to over-extending his back legs and over-reaching. However, if the over-reaching is not due to the over-extension of the hind limbs but the slow breakover of the front feet, longer heels and rolled toes will help to speed up the breakover.

Any shoe being pulled off can potentially cause damage to the hoof. If your horse is prone to over-reaching, let your farrier know (if he doesn't notice himself!). He will be able to set the back shoes slightly back of the toes so that, if the horse does tread on his own front heels, he will strike with hoof and not steel, diminishing the chances of severe damage being sustained. Above all, never blame your farrier if a shoe is lost. If the shoe has got so thin that it has worn through and fallen off, then you should have called in the farrier earlier. If your horse pulls a shoe off, it is bad luck, but highly unlikely to be a result of something that the farrier has done. Endurance horses are shod to prevent this sort of problem occurring, with wide-webbed, welded, rolled toe shoes with support at the heels and a tungsten nail at the back corners of the front shoes, and wide-webbed shoes set a quarter of an inch back at the toes of the hinds, with perhaps an additional tungsten nail on the outside back corner.

The most common but consistently irritating problem in an endurance horse's action is brushing with the back feet, and even a horse with normally clear movement may start to brush as he tires. Needless

The farrier at work. This is one of the people on whom you rely to keep your horse fit to compete, so it is worth finding, and keeping, the right person.

to say, there is a chance of an injury occurring whenever one foot strikes its opposite foot or leg. Keep an eye on the insides of your horse's hind feet and legs for tell-tale marks. Your farrier may be able to set the back shoes under a little on the inside and slightly out on the outside. This will alter the centre of balance in the foot and the placement of the foot on the ground. The alteration in the flight of the feet to a barely perceptible extent visually may, however, be just enough to prevent the onset of brushing.

Forging (striking the underside of the front shoe with the hinds) can also occur in horses that become tired, but this is largely up to the rider to rectify. As with over-reaching, setting the hind shoes back slightly will ensure that only horn hits the front feet and not steel, which should mean that bruising to the front feet, if it is sustained at all, will be minimal. Soles that are prone to bruising can be protected by the use of pads, which today are commonly made of a soft, shock-absorbent plastic. Many riders routinely fit these to their horses whenever they are going to compete over flinty areas. It is worthwhile taking advice from your farrier over pads and filling, as unless very carefully fitted, there is a risk of grit finding its way between the pad and the sole and causing problems.

Starting work

When you intend to start competing in endurance, ask your farrier to make up a spare set of your horse's shoes, or keep a barely-worn pair from a previous shoeing. It saves time, hassle and money if you always have a spare set with you at rides, in case a shoe is pulled off or is worn dangerously thin. Ride farriers will often be able to meet you at a vet gate or checkpoint and nail the spare shoe back on, eliminating any risk of working with an unprotected foot. Horses who pull shoes off on rides are often successfully re-shod and continue to pass vettings perfectly sound and well.

Many riders also take some kind of protective hoof boot with them to put on in case a farrier is unable to reach them. I have never had much success with these when out on the trail as they can be fiddly to put on securely without the help of an assistant. Today, checkpoints are so frequent and radio contact so good that you will rarely have an excessively long wait, or need to ride a long way without a shoe. As long as your horse's foot has not been badly damaged or the terrain is not dangerously flinty, your horse should be able to continue steadily for several miles with no ill-effects.

Ride farriers always have to check your horse's feet before you start, and if you know that you have work to be done, it is inconsiderate and time-wasting to demand attention unless you have had absolutely no other option. If you aren't going to a ride with shoes just a few days old and you have clenches which need tightening, arrive early and ask the farrier if he would be able to attend to them. It is unfair to expect other competitors to be held up on your behalf. It is always a good idea to have your horse shod during the week before a ride, affording the best chance for wear but giving you a couple of days to bed them in and give your horse a chance to get used to the shoes.

The worst problems likely to occur to your horse's feet during a ride, apart from pulling off a shoe, will be sustaining a puncture wound or a

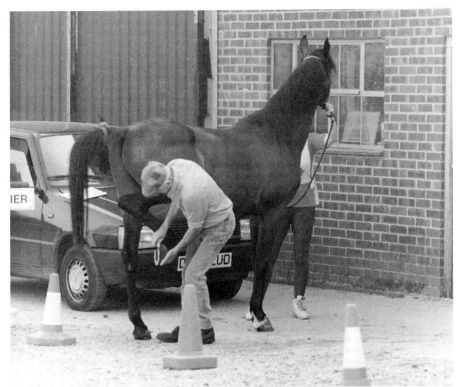

Checking feet before a ride. The ride farrier is there to make sure that your horse's feet are well shod and likely to go the distance, not to do a complete re-fit!

stone bruise. We will discuss how to cope with these in the chapter on injuries. At the end of each competitive season when your horse has his holiday, his hooves will appreciate the break, too. If your horse's feet are of good enough quality, he may appreciate going without shoes for a month or two to grow the nail-holes out, just being trimmed every four weeks. If this is not possible, have a lighter set of shoes put on, as the weight reduction will assist horn strength and regeneration. With a skilful farrier and considerate stable management, your horse's feet should be able to reach their potential and cope well with the season's workload.

3

Basic Schooling and Education

Once upon a time, horses were a major form of transport and their riders were nothing more than passengers and drivers. However, if you choose to compete with your horse, you must treat him not as transport, but as an athlete, with whom you will work in partnership. Even during a competitive ride of short mileage, you and your horse need to travel together for many hours, at a good speed, sometimes over treacherous terrain. Sustained travel means that economy is the watchword in terms of energy expenditure and, to conserve energy, minimum effort should be used for propulsion. Whenever you ride, you and your horse should work together as a team, in a balanced way. It is impossible for your horse to conserve his energy or even to move easily and freely with a rider lurching about on top, so you have to give him the optimum opportunity to work effectively. The longer the period that you are in the saddle, the more difficult it becomes to sustain this harmony, yet the more important it becomes that you do so. In this chapter, we will examine how you can improve your ability to work together in an efficient and economical way.

Initial health care

Before you can even think about getting your horse fit enough to take part in an endurance ride you need to consider his basic health. The well-being of the animal is the primary concern in this sport and preparation is the key to producing a horse in competition condition. Without some initial groundwork, there is little point in even thinking about getting your horse fit enough to compete. The first step is to give him a basic health check to make sure that he is in good shape. He should be wormed, have up-to-date vaccinations, well-kept teeth, be sound and have no obvious health or physical problems. A healthy horse should have a glossy coat that lies flat. If it is staring or patchy, he could be harbouring parasites such as worms or lice, which need to be treated for his general health to improve.

Ideally, you should also make a photographic record of his musculature in his current state. In this way, as he improves with work, you will be able to assess his development through comparison. It is also helpful to get an idea of his starting weight, using a tape. A horse carrying lots of extra fat will need to whittle down gradually before you ask him to do much athletic work; conversely, a horse in poor condition, who needs building up, should not be asked to over-exert himself until you have an idea of the level that he is capable of working at. If you have any suspicion that your horse is not in the best of health and ready to start working, have your vet take a blood test, which will shed light on any abnormalities.

Metabolic parameters

Next, acquaint yourself with your horse's metabolic parameters in an unfit state so that you will be able to monitor progress during training. You need a few basic tools in order to be able to do this: a thermometer should always be included in your tack box, and a stethoscope makes life so much easier. The basic parameters to monitor are his temperature, pulse and respiration rates. Getting used to your own horse's rates is the key to fitness training and general care at home, and management throughout every ride.

Temperature is always taken the same way; the norm is 38°C/100.4°F with half a degree either way considered as normal daily variation. Temperature is a valuable diagnostic aid to your horse's well-being: if he is off colour or appears unwell, significant changes in his temperature can be the first confirmation you will have that there is a problem.

Your horse's pulse rate can be taken with your fingers at various points, the most accessible being the large vein that runs underneath the jaw or at the back of the pastern. However, a stethoscope makes the task simple and once you can locate a pulse in this way, you will be able to find it on any horse. Place the drum of the stethoscope against the horse's girth area, a little forward of where the girth would sit, just behind the left elbow. Each heart beat is heard as a double bump, as the heart pumps in and out. The rhythm should be regular and strong, without dropping beats or pounding erratically. If you look at your watch and count with the beats you will get a good idea if they are even (i.e. every second or couple of seconds) or irregular. The normal range at rest is anywhere between 30 and 44 beats per minute; occasionally in a fit horse it may drop below 30.

It can also be helpful to monitor your horse's respiration rate, either by watching your horse's sides move in and out with each breath, or by laying a hand on his side to feel each breath, if that is easier. This way you will get used to his resting rates and working rates (resting is usually 8-14 breaths per minute) and you will know if he is breathing irregularly

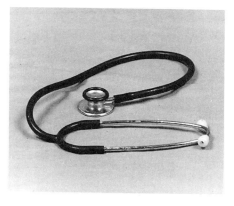

Above: Stethoscope.

Right: Taking the pulse with a stethoscope and stopwatch. You need to be able to find your horse's pulse points quickly and familiarise yourself with his metabolic rates.

or panting hard. Each breath should be quiet, even and regular. If he is dragging or forcing each breath, there may be an allergic or other wind problem which needs to be treated.

Ride education

Once you are satisfied that your horse is physically sound and well, you can begin to think about his education in preparation for schooling and training. Background preparation for competition can be thought of in terms of education and adaptability. You can educate your horse at home to cope with many of the situations that you will meet on a ride. You can teach him to get used to being met by a crew out in the open, having his feet picked out while you are on top, and being sponged down or sloshed from a bottle. You can do this while he is standing still, back at the yard, from the ground or the saddle. It is helpful to give him the opportunity to drink from a bucket offered by a helper, as he will need to do this on a ride. It can take a while for horses to relax enough to drink freely at a ride, so any groundwork you can do at home gives you a head start.

You also need to teach him, in the comfort of his own yard, to get used to being vetted. Ask other people to come and perform an imitation vetting on your horse, including looking in his mouth, running hands up and down his legs and back, and taking his pulse. He must learn to stand still and behave for the vets at a ride, and should not be concerned about being handled by strangers. Practise trotting out, for around 30 metres/yards, round a cone or other marker. He needs to trot with and without tack on, at a good rhythm, on a loose rein. The handler should never interfere with the horse's action; give the horse a couple of feet of rope or rein and jog beside him, not in front, which will hamper the vet's view.

Teach him to slow down to your voice as he approaches each end of the trot-up, so that you don't need to interfere with his head. Always turn him away from you when rounding the marker, again so that you don't interfere with what the vet can see. Get him used to being trotted in both a headcollar and bridle; the rules change periodically and vary according to what stage of a ride you are at. It is also useful to teach your prospective crew to do a good trot-up with the horse. Many people just don't know how to trot a horse out well, which makes the ride vet's job more difficult and can result in wasted time through requests for repeat performances.

Learning to trust each other

In preparation for situations that you may come across in open country, you need to give your horse some background in versatility. You need to establish a firm bond of trust in each other at home, which will enable

The perfect trot-up: relaxed horse and handler, a good length of rein, steady speed and the rider running beside the horse to allow the vets to see the horse move.

Teaching your horse to cope with situations that he might meet on a ride is excellent preparation. There are plenty of horses who are reluctant to cross water until they learn that it really is safe.

you to cope with strange or difficult situations on a ride. It is important that you trust your horse to go anywhere and give his utmost in any situation, and that he trusts you not to lead him into danger. In this way, you will be able to meet with confidence any eventuality during your riding career.

During a ride, you will encounter certain situations in which you may require extra co-operation and even help from your horse. Again, you can give him a head start at home by going out to meet this kind of situation whenever possible. He will need to cope with passing other horses, being passed by them, and learning to let other horses approach him from other directions without worrying. If you can ride occasionally in a busy area with other horses, he will be mentally more relaxed in a competitive situation. You must be able to manage him alone and in company as, during a ride, you may have to go first, last, alone or in a pack. Many horses become attached to others that they meet and work with during a ride, which can make vettings difficult for all concerned.

Take your horse to places where he will have to walk over bridges, ditches, streams and other obstacles in his path. If he isn't confident, ask him to at least be brave enough to follow you across. Educating the horse to act and react quickly to cues from you and the environment can be done whilst out training and in the paddock or manège at home. Show jumping and lungeing over poles with different stride lengths or numbers of strides between them will encourage him to think quickly. He will also become accustomed to having to react to obstacles underfoot. This sort of training comes into its own when out on the trail, dodging ruts, stones, logs and other objects, picking the best ground and moving quickly across tracks and so on. Practise opening and closing gates from your horse's back; this is a valuable skill which will save you both lots of time, trouble and energy during a ride.

Rider as trainer

As you are the person who will be competing with your horse, you are really the only person who can work with your horse and teach him to deal with riding hazards. In order to be able to go out and meet new challenges together, you need your horse to work efficiently. To produce him effectively yourself, you need to assess your horse's current level of schooling, training and ability. More importantly, you need to be able to examine yourself in the same objective manner. Honestly assessing your own riding ability is not an easy task. Even to the technically minded, it isn't easy to pick up nuances in posture and weight placement in both horse and rider. However, it is precisely these slight changes that make the difference between a team working in equilibrium and one that struggles. As you are going to compete together, you need to improve together.

In an ideal world we would all have an experienced trainer on tap, but the reality is generally that you need to be competent and dedicated enough to train yourself and your own horse. You need to help him, as he will have problems in maintaining his own balance if you are not able to take responsibility for your own. A vast number of riders who have 'learned to ride' and have owned their own horse for many years, believe that they are good riders. However, none of us is beyond improvement, and admitting this is essential if you are to become more effective and efficient, and better able to help your horse cope with the demands which you place on him. Most of us develop bad habits which, during the course of a long ride, can make life very difficult for our horses. Any postural problems that you have will set up resistances and imbalances in your horse, so it is vital that you concentrate on your own riding before you expect your horse to perform properly.

Rider balance

If you have a tendency to tip forward, slouch, or collapse a hip, your horse will be struggling against that imbalance and will attempt to maintain his equilibrium by compensating for your problems. Just as there are few perfect horses, there are few perfect riders, and practice is the key to improvement. As your horse reacts to your instructions, you also need to be able to react to his movements. If he shies, lengthens or shortens a stride, stumbles or makes a change of speed, you should be able to help him recover and not add to the problem, or worse still, fall off! If you are working alone, gather as many photographs of yourself in action as you can, or ask someone to video you riding at every pace, over jumps, round corners and on rough ground. This way you will be able to see your own habits and problems and work on them. Ask a friend to lunge you, without stirrups or reins, or better still, bareback. Riding as many different horses as you can will make you a more effective and useful rider, not just one whose horse is used to your aids and methods.

Posture and bad habits

Concentrate on your posture, and on keeping yourself in balance with your horse. Your weight should stay central and flexible, without tipping forward or back or to one side. You should ride quietly and in a poised way, without bodily movement that is out of 'sync' with what your horse is doing. Your head should be supported above your neck and not tipping your weight forwards, backwards or to the side. Your shoulders and hips should be level, not collapsing either way. Your spine should be flexible, to absorb the horse's motion, but always perpendicular.

Your body weight should fall as much through your legs as possible, which will give you a secure seat over rough ground. Most recreational riders have a tendency to keep their weight in their seats, sitting like a passenger in a car, with their legs in front. Imagine yourself standing up: your legs cannot be of any use in supporting your weight unless they are underneath you! They should stay long, not folded up or rigidly jutting out to the sides or in other directions. If your feet point to the front and not out at right angles, you will suffer less strain to your calf muscles and lower back. Your arms and hands should stay close to your body and not flail all over the place. Some rider's elbows look fit to take flight at canter, which can only result in a hard hand jerking on the horse's mouth, not giving as he extends his head and neck.

Useful schooling

Having identified your own shortcomings, you need to identify those of your horse. Again, videos and photographs are helpful, as is lungeing or

watching someone else ride your horse. It is encouraging that there is a potential for vast improvement in most horses' way of going through schooling techniques. The aim is to achieve the ideal state of economical, balanced yet dynamic motion. Again, most horses work in a way that is far from ideal! You will probably know which side and which leg your horse favours from your own experience of riding him. A horse who resists on one rein or leg or particularly favours one side is likely to be responding to your riding and, with a different rider, may favour the other leg or rein. However, prolonged resistances set up imbalances in muscular development and over a period of time your horse may actually find it easier to work one way than the other.

Watch how your horse moves on bends – motorbiking round corners is a common fault and is partly due to habit on the horse's part. However, a leaning rider encourages the horse to drop his shoulder underneath and throw his weight to the inside. Learn to use your head, shoulders, hips and legs to keep the horse vertical around corners. His body should follow his head and stay upright – a horse who throws his weight to the inside on a sharp bend is unlikely to stay on his feet on slippery tarmac or in deep, boggy going. Teaching a horse to corner correctly will depend upon your weight being in the right place, so hold yourself up. Some lateral work will teach him to move away from your

The typical way of going for an endurance horse and rider: long, low and relaxed, but with the horse in self-carriage and well balanced.

leg, which is vital in working situations. All of this might sound very dull and technical, but once you are out on the trail, you need a supple, balanced horse. Preparation of this kind will help him to stay upright in difficult situations and react instantly to your cues. The versatile, supple horse will be able to move away from your leg to enable you to open gates quickly, avoid hazards and move off rough ground. He will also be able to corner efficiently, particularly at speed.

The engine at the back

To equip your horse with the necessary musculature to begin endurance training, you need to aim for balance, suppleness and muscular strength. The basic design of the equine skeleton means that it automatically travels on its forehand, carrying the heavy head and neck first with the lighter quarters following. Add to that the rider's weight and, as you will know if you have backed or worked with a young horse, the animal's natural tendency is to pull himself along from the front. However, this is the least efficient way for a horse to travel. A horse that works on his forehand will tire quickly, and is unlikely to have much success with hill work. Travelling downhill with the back end trailing, not acting to support and steady the load, will mean that the pair of you are likely to overbalance. Any horse pulling the entire weight of his own body, and yours, using mainly his front legs, will have difficulty working at or sustaining any speed. Therefore, your horse needs to learn to bring his back end underneath himself and use his hindquarters and back legs as his primary motor.

Economy of energy

By muscling up and suppling your horse's back end, you can teach him to use himself correctly and vastly improve his way of going. You can provide him with the freedom to move in a balanced, economical and ground-covering way and motor along with all his propulsion coming from the back. The long-term aim is to teach your horse to travel using a constant, regular, low level of impulsion. Using his back end will enable you to lighten and free up the front which, in turn, will give your horse's shoulder the freedom to extend and move with a longer, looser stride. The amount of impulsion that you can create and the collection that you can maintain during any schooling work will depend not only upon your riding ability, but also upon your horse's conformation. Horses with very long back legs, or with very upright hind-limb conformation will have difficulty bringing their hocks and quarters underneath.

The rider's ability to channel impulsion from the hindquarters is vital, then, to enable the endurance horse to do his job well. However, there are no short cuts. This is not a simple task and it requires a fit and capable rider. The correct development will not come just through pulling from the front to round up your horse's outline. He needs to be worked through from the back, creating impulsion and then using your hands, seat, back and legs to gently keep the lid on the bubbling pan. Working a horse in this way should never result in a solid, tense neck, a set jaw and a pounding stride. Any resistance indicates a physical problem, pain, or bad riding. There should be no resistance, but a mouth as light as a feather, a poised outline with the horse in self-carriage, and legs like springs. This sort of result will not come instantly. As you will know yourself, suddenly using muscles which are under-developed and unaccustomed to working is not easy. If your horse is not used to working in an outline or using himself correctly, minimal steps need to be taken at a time to produce steady, gradual progress. His musculature must be gently developed to prevent the risk of soreness or stiffness, which creates resistance and defeats the entire object of the exercise.

Other training strategies

All of this sounds as though you are expected to ride everywhere in a collected, bouncing outline. This, of course, is not true, but work that you do in improving your horse's way of going will enable him to travel in a balanced way on a loose rein. On a ride, you need to be able to ride him with little or no contact at all, leaving his head and neck free to pick his going and avoid hazards. He should also respond to the lightest of aids, using as little of your energy as possible. Ideally, you should be able to move him from one piece of ground to another using your legs alone. In practice, this is not the case with a fresh, fit animal working at speed.

However, you can provide yourself with extra help by teaching him to halt from leg and seat. In an emergency, this will prevent you having to yank on his mouth – if this happens, he will inevitably throw his head up in the air and lose balance.

Western training

Apart from ordinary ridden schooling, employing some Western techniques can be helpful. The ability to neck-rein, for example, is invaluable out on the trail, particularly when working at speed. It actually only takes a few minutes to teach your horse this technique and is best done in an enclosed area, but you can practise while you are out hacking. You should start out by using your legs to guide his direction, placing the weight of the reins against the horse's neck on the side that you want him to turn away from. You may well find that your hand/eye co-ordination has a faster reaction than your legs and seat, so turning your horse quickly away from the rein can be really helpful.

Using the voice

Training your horse to respond to your voice is also a good idea. You will often hear endurance riders chatting away to their horses out on the trail, and it isn't always just for the sake of companionship! It is useful to have a horse who is responsive to commands like 'Steady', 'Whoa', 'Trot', 'Walk', and 'Stand'. These commands are useful to reinforce the other aids, and save a great deal of physical energy if they will work alone.

All of these ideas will help to make you and your horse better equipped for endurance training. Once your horse has some basic education and schooling for the task in hand, you can begin to think about getting him fit to compete. In reality, the processes of education and schooling will not take place in isolation, but will be incorporated into your programme of work as you prepare your horse for a ride. In the next chapter, we will look at the workload, and how you are likely to go about producing a horse fit enough to cope with endurance riding.

4

Conditioning for Competition

Endurance riding is a test of fitness, and to be successful a very fit horse is required. Flat-racing sprinters are extremely fit, but would be unlikely to complete an endurance ride. As the sport takes the form of sustained, low-level exercise, an endurance horse needs a completely different kind of fitness. He needs to be equipped to work at a steady speed, for a long period, with the minimum risk of fatigue. The difference in these 'kinds of fitness' is as a result of the way in which a horse has been conditioned. Your endurance horse will be not a short-distance, 100-metre sprinter, with chunky muscles and a system trained to produce short bursts of energy; instead he is the marathon runner of the equine world. Light-weight, tough and powerful muscles are needed to propel an endurance horse, muscles that use the minimum of energy and cast off as much heat as possible. He must have a cardiovascular system that works efficiently to fuel these muscles and, most importantly of all, he needs to be adequately prepared to cope with the demands placed upon him.

You are aiming to produce a supremely fit, laid-back equine athlete in the peak of physical condition. When you begin to demand more of your horse, whose mundane, easy workload consists of, say, a stroll round the block at weekends, your approach to his management has to change correspondingly. You need to put in an appropriate level of work and keep him according to his new needs. You would not expect to be able to run a marathon yourself without careful preparation, and the same applies to preparing an endurance horse. In the last chapter, we examined basic health care as a preliminary to getting a horse fit. Now you are going to condition your horse for endurance, you must begin by managing him accordingly.

Stable management

To start with, you cannot expect your horse's system to function to the best of its ability if it is at a disadvantage. Therefore, his stable management must be geared to athletic work. Any dust in his atmosphere will impair his performance by preventing his lungs from working to capacity, so make sure that he is kept on a good, deep bed of clean, bright straw or, if necessary, on a dust-free bedding. To maintain a dust-free regime, his hay should be soaked, or you may need to switch to a dust-free forage.

Your horse's home environment should be as hazard-free as you can make it, as you don't want to risk unnecessary injury. A horse who is out working for more of the time will come home and relax with a good roll, so make sure that the ground in his paddock is safe. Large rocks, bricks and foreign objects which may scratch or harm your horse should be picked up. Even cast shoes can cause nasty scratches! A fit horse also has a tendency to exercise himself and may become more clumsy than before. If he is intent on going out and cantering several laps of his field each day before settling down to eat, he may skid into fences or round corners, so make sure that there is nothing there which could potentially cause an injury.

Individual management

Care of the equine athlete at home involves not only careful stable management, but sensitive management of the individual himself. While you are working your horse you need to look him over every day and develop a manager's eye for his well-being, both physical and mental, and his development and progress. By routine you should run your hands down his legs morning, evening and after he has been working. The primary point of this is to feel for signs of exercise-induced stress, but it also acts as a therapeutic massage for the structures within the leg.

First, feel the legs with a light touch that travels gently over the leg, allowing the flat of your hand to detect any heat. Hot spots are the primary indication of further trouble through inflammation, or an influx of blood to a site where damage has occurred. Feel for any swelling or puffiness; you will become accustomed to the difference between the hard, tight swellings that occur as a result of injury and the soft swellings that contain no heat but appear as a result of the filling of the lymph glands or a sluggish circulation, such as wind galls. You will also be able to pick up any nicks, cuts or abrasions that are on the skin which may be hidden by the horse's hair.

Anything abnormal should be dealt with accordingly, by consulting your vet if necessary, or through treatment or rest. Cuts and abrasions are easily dealt with, but if your horse's legs are not able to cope with the level of work you are giving him, you need to back-track a stage or two. He may well require some rest, before resuming exercise at a lower level and building up again gradually. Plenty of horses enjoy working to the point where they will quite happily overdo it, and the legs are the first place where such stresses will show. With practice, you will learn how to read your horse and his capacity for work and be able to prevent this point from being reached. However, with careful preparation, your horse's legs should stay sound and be capable of handling a workload that is built up in easy stages. Recurring injury of the same type is likely to point to an underlying weakness and should be thoroughly investigated before continuing with any programme of work.

Troubleshooting

Following the same principles of observation, the horse's general well-being should be carefully monitored in the same way. If you can, watch him when he is relaxed and at rest. Ten minutes spent observing him over the stable door in the evenings will assist you in knowing what is his general demeanour and what is unusual. For example, if he rests a leg or points a toe, is it a normal habit for him, or an early warning of a strain or pain somewhere? Habits such as these may indicate pain higher up the leg, in the back or elsewhere in the body, or may be an indication of discomfort in the foot. Feet should be checked over daily and a close eye kept on their condition and that of the shoes. Look for signs of cracking and chipping of the horn, foreign bodies wedged anywhere, bruising to the soles and uneven wear to the shoes. Lots of work can cause concussive problems to the feet, and deterioration of the horn can result quite quickly if preventive measures are not taken early enough.

The condition of his skin should be monitored in the same way. Rubbing and chafing can occur in any horse, but particularly in thin-skinned horses. The skin may have had insufficient time to toughen up and become accustomed to constant wear from tack, or may be suffering from sweat rash. Constant sweating will dry out sensitive areas of the skin and produce flaking, partly the result of bacterial action. The girth area is particularly prone to itchy sweat-rash as the girth concentrates so much pressure in such a small surface area of sensitive skin.

Clipping him may help to keep his skin in better condition as the sweat can evaporate freely and won't become trapped by body hair. At higher mileage levels, endurance horses are often kept clipped out during the competitive season to minimise retained heat; it also helps to keep them comfortable. His skin provides a valuable means of testing for dehydration. At a ride, you will often see vets pinching a fold of skin at the base of the neck and timing the number of seconds it takes to return to normal afterwards. Ideally, skin should spring back to normal straight away, and the longer it takes, the more dehydrated the horse is – three or more seconds indicates the onset of dehydration.

The horse's metabolic parameters, in particular his pulse, should be monitored as part of your routine management during any exercise programme. Throughout your training, take his pulse rate at rest following

A fit, happy horse. Observation and knowing your horse are the keys to maintaining his well-being.

exercise, ideally after 30 minutes. It should always fall to his resting rate, or at the very least below 64bpm, which is the elimination limit at a ride. In practice it is likely to reach his resting rate, and if you monitor his pulse every 5 minutes you will get a much better idea of how quickly he is actually recovering from the work you are asking him to do.

Warming up and cooling down

Before you commence with a training programme, it is essential to ensure that your horse is properly warmed up and cooled down either side of the workout. Before you start any work faster than a walk, you should have your horse walking actively for at least 10 minutes to ensure that his muscles are warmed through and loosened up. Trotting should start gently and be carried out for a good 5 minutes further to this before asking for increased activity or speed at trot, or any canter work. Before a gallop, your horse should be properly warmed through for an absolute minimum of 20 minutes. Prior to a long ride or one that is known to be over fast terrain, you will often see horses warming up, starting from a gentle walk and progressing through to a steady canter.

Cooling down should involve, ideally, a mile of steady walking towards home in training or at the end of a ride. If you have a very hot horse

A well-matched combination working happily together. This pony is going to need careful cooling after the ride.

following a training session, keep him walking until he is cool and almost dry. During a ride and at home in the summer, you can use lots of water to keep your horse cool, but never throw water over a horse who is anything less than hot. Always warm your water on a cold day and never return from a ride, soak a horse and then 'park' it. The key to cooling down is that is should be done actively. To keep muscles cool and loose, the blood should be kept moving through the veins, to carry away waste products and receive the cooling effects of water. It is normal to soak a horse's neck whilst his quarters are rugged, as it is so important to keep the large muscles warm whilst gradually cooling out the blood.

Early conditioning

Much careful and instinctive management is essential when conditioning a horse for competition. A horse who undergoes a fitness programme goes through a series of changes and if you have never had a very fit horse, you will be amazed and delighted in his new streamlined appearance. If you have got horses fit for other disciplines, you may need to rethink your ideas and adapt them to this different form of sport. Preparing your horse for endurance is essentially a process of gradually conditioning his system to become accustomed to the work which you are going to demand of it. Your long-term aim is to produce a body that is equipped to cope with the stresses that it meets in competition. Next to sound legs and feet and a strong heart and lungs, your horse needs muscles which can sustain steady work for long periods of time.

The technical story

Muscles are enabled to work through tissue respiration or breathing, which takes place when blood oxygen reaches the tissue. However, the work of the muscle is fuelled by energy, either from blood glucose or muscle glycogen. The entire working process is made possible by a high-energy compound called adenosine triphosphate or ATP, within the body cells. During any form of muscular activity, the ATP energy is used, with heat as a by-product. This reduces the ATP to ADP, adenosine diphosphate, which has to be returned (through breaking down sugar) to its triphosphate form to enable work to continue. When oxygen from the blood is unavailable or insufficient to fuel the process, anaerobic tissue respiration occurs. This does not entirely break down sugar and a build-up of lactic acid occurs, which in turn prevents ATP from being regenerated, causing fatigue and possibly azoturia.

Oxygen is obviously one of the vital ingredients in preventing lactic acid build-up, and in carrying it away when it is produced. When the horse's system tells him it's reaching overload, he will naturally slow up and blow hard, to try and replace the oxygen debt. In training a horse or getting him fit, what you are actually doing is training his entire system to become more efficient. The endurance horse's circulatory system will progressively respond to oxygen demand within the muscles by forming extra capillaries to carry that oxygen in the blood. His ability to use and carry oxygen increases in this way, and his respiration rate will lower accordingly. His heart rate becomes lower and he will work at an overall lower rate, which will gradually recover more quickly after exercise.

Getting fitter

Fitness training can therefore be considered to begin from the point when the endurance horse's muscles are asked to do more work. There are two muscle fibre types, slow and fast twitch, which contract at the speeds their names suggest. Literally, slow-twitch fibres are used for slow work, and fast twitch for fast work. For endurance, horses need a pre-dominance of slow-twitch muscle fibres. The primary difference between the two types of fibre is the way in which they work and use fuel; slow twitch muscle contracts slowly, but uses oxygen to burn glycogen (i.e. it works aerobically).

Endurance training therefore seeks to improve the horse's glycogen conservation, and develop his slow-twitch muscle fibres. It is claimed that this type of conditioning can take place within a fairly short period – that a horse can be got fit enough to compete in a 20-mile ride within six to eight weeks from completely soft condition. However, there are no short cuts, and I prefer to allow ten or twelve weeks and work slowly towards fitness. If your horse is doing a fair amount of work already, he may be able to compete in a 20-mile ride tomorrow with perfect ease. To assess his level of fitness, compare the work he is currently doing to each stage in the following guide to preparation. It must be stressed that this is purely a guide and that each horse will vary; some horses love work and are easy to get fit, others take longer.

Stage 1: Walking

The best way to start this kind of conditioning work is, as with any elementary fitness training, by walking. If you are bringing up a completely unfit horse, you should start by walking for just 20 or 30 minutes a day. Ask your horse to walk actively, with a long, loose stride, at a reasonable pace. As he begins to cope more easily, increase the work by 10 minutes every few days until he is walking easily for an hour. In a completely unfit horse or novice youngster, this may take you up to three weeks. Trying to hurry the process will only result in the risk of injury and stress, incurring lay-offs and having to start all over again. At this stage, his work should be over fairly flat, even ground, but not necessarily roads. Once he is coping well on easy going, start to make use of any hills in your area by walking up them, on a contact, encouraging your horse to use his back end. This will help to build up muscles throughout his hindquarters and teach him to work through from behind, not pull himself along from in front. You are aiming to have him walking actively for an hour, five days a week.

Stage 2: The trot

Once he is walking well, you can start to introduce some periods of trot. Initially keep it to a steady, working trot for fairly short periods of time. You may find that your horse will blow or sweat if he is unaccustomed to work, so don't ask too much of him at this stage. You should not ask him to sustain a trot for more than a couple of minutes at a time, with a maximum of 10 minutes' overall trotting during an hour's total work time. Whilst you can continue to ask him to walk up hills, it is best at this stage to trot gently on the flat. You can gradually increase his overall exercise time to 1 hour 15 minutes, then 1 1/2 hours, five days a week. It may have taken you between four and six weeks to reach this stage. There are no hard-and-fast rules. Be wary of allowing a horse who loves

A real travelling trot. The horse knows the job, is moving freely and covering the ground. If the rider had a slightly longer leg position she would be better centred over the horse and make the job even easier.

work to over-exert himself, as you may find that physical stresses occur as a result of the excitement.

Stages 3–5: Progressive work

Once he is coping comfortably with $1^1/_2$ hours, including 10 minutes at a trot, you can increase the trotting work gradually to 20 minutes. At this stage you can ask him to do some gentle schooling on the flat and to begin extending his stride for short periods of time. Again, once he is coping with this level of work, you can ask him to trot gently up some hills in a controlled way as part of his allotted trotting time (stage 4). This is probably around week seven, eight or later. Again, ask him to use himself, not just attack the hills and pull himself up from in front. Stage 5 is to keep the level of trotting work constant but again increase the time that he works for, gradually up to 1 hour 45 minutes five days a week. You may be including up to 20 minutes of gentle schooling or lungeing as part of his trotting time.

Stage 6: Approaching fitness

Once he has become accustomed to working for a longer period, increase the time spent trotting again. In this way, you are gradually increasing the distance he covers, initially by walking further for a longer period of time, then by increasing the trot but maintaining the time for which he is ridden. The general scheme is to increase the time spent working at a slower speed every time before adding any more time at a faster speed,

A nicely balanced pair and a fairly collected canter. The canter is a pace at which many horses travel most naturally and economically, though not always in such a rounded outline.

or adding speed in itself. You may now ask him to keep up an extended trot for slightly longer or, if he prefers to canter, introducing some gentle, balanced canter work for not more than 5 minutes overall initially. Now his trotting work can gradually be built up to 30 minutes, including some gentle cantering, lungeing, schooling, or jumping. Your workouts can be increased to 2 hours by extending your walking time. By this time, roughly week ten to twelve, your horse should be fairly fit and his most basic level of physical work has now been established.

Stage 7: Establishing a maintenance rate

At this stage, a change in strategy is called for. You are unlikely to have the time to work your horse for 2 hours, five days a week, and your horse may well become bored with the routine. Here I would advocate a change in programme according to your individual horse's physical and psychological needs. He still needs to work five days a week, with two days' rest. Now that he is fit, you may find that he will work for up to $2^{1}/_{2}$ hours one day at a fairly good pace, in which case he should only work gently for an hour or 90 minutes the following day. One day you might like to lunge steadily for 30-40 minutes; one day you might school him on the flat to increase his suppleness for an hour, or have a lesson; one day you might go out for a fast workout just for an hour; one day you might spend popping over jumps. You might like to box to a beach, steeper hills, or a different area to ride in for a change of terrain and scenery.

Hill work

Hill work is probably the most useful aid to fitness, and if there are no hills in your area it is advisable to box to some and use them for work. Lots of steady walking up and down hills with the horse using himself properly, should help to develop the right muscles behind and keep the weight there. Trotting up hills, and later cantering up them, forces the whole system to work harder than it does on the flat. There is nothing like it for muscling up and giving the cardiovascular system a workout! Personally I would never ride any faster than a steady jog downhill in training; on a ride, though, you may need to go faster to make up time. It is said that horses trained in very flat areas have difficulty coping with hills. Whilst this is not uniformly true in terms of actual fitness, it does make a difference mentally. Some horses find hills quite daunting and it is unfair to expect your horse to cope with difficult terrain if he is unprepared for it. The best endurance rides are run in areas of the country with really testing terrain, so it is worth making an effort to cover every eventuality in training.

Pacing

Whatever your own personal system, once he is coping with an average of 2 hours' steady work five days a week he should be easily coping with his first rides. To complete your first ride you will need to gradually become accustomed to your horse's speed at each pace. As a general rule, a horse walks at 5-6mph, trots at 7-12mph and canters at 9-14mph. Much above 14mph is a fast canter or slower gallop. Obviously the easiest method for speed gauging is to ride your horse along a measured mile in variations of each pace, and time how long it takes to cover that mile. Ideally, you should hit your measured stretch during a longer period of work, as just starting and stopping will not give a realistic picture of your horse's average speed in each pace.

It is thought that the most economical pace for a horse, in terms of energy expenditure, is a gentle canter; some horses prefer to trot, some naturally canter. Endurance horses with a few seasons behind them tend to begin to canter naturally the more experienced they become. Allow your horse to work in his favourite pace; he has chosen it because it feels best to him. Remember to keep changing legs and diagonals in order to prevent one set of muscles from becoming tired.

First rides

If you would like to be sure of his level of fitness, practice a 15- or 20-mile route before you enter a ride, either at home or by boxing out to a different area. You should be aiming to complete at around 7mph, which is the speed you will need to ride at in competition. You should try to work at a steady trot, walking the last half mile home. You may have the odd stretch of gentle canter, do some walking, or stop to cross roads or open or close gates.

Have a mock vetting afterwards – take your horse's pulse around 30 minutes after finishing. Practise trotting him up, too – you need to know if he has managed to stay sound! You are unlikely to have to do much cooling out after 20 miles, and will probably only need to scrape off the mud. Keep your horse walking gently, to prevent him getting stiff during the time before your practice vetting. In reality, if you have been working your horse at home for around $2^{1}/_{2}$ hours including half an hour or more in trot, you have probably covered around 13 to 15 miles anyway.

Some endurance riders use every weekend as the opportunity for a long training ride at home. I never usually ride much more than 15 miles in training and, once your horse has established a basic physical level of fitness, it is unnecessary to keep clocking up miles unless, of course, you both desperately want to. Believe it or not, you have now completed the most difficult part of your horse's fitness programme! Once he has completed a 20-mile ride, you need to reinforce and build on his existing

In early rides, your horse should simply be kept fit enough to enjoy his work, rather than too lean or over-trained.

level of fitness in order to prepare him to progress through each level. Remember that a marathon runner will not practise by running 26 miles every Saturday – the result would be overwork. You can start to ask him to increase his speed slightly or to trot for longer periods at home which will give his heart and lungs a better work-out. Keep him ticking over at the same level, perhaps occasionally riding for $2^{1}/_{2}$ hours and incorporating more hills into your route.

Increasing distance

Once you are both coping easily with 20- or 25-mile rides, try a 30-mile ride. Once horses have got the hang of competing they rarely notice a slight increase in mileage. Thirty miles is the longest ride that you will do without stopping for a vetting in some form. You need regular crewing and lots of positive thinking, as this can be quite a barrier for both of you. Once you can both cope with 30 miles with ease, go up to 40 miles. A 40-mile ride is simply a 20-mile ride twice, with a break for vetting in the middle, and often involves riding two laps of the same route. When setting out on the second lap, ask your horse to leave the half-way venue positively and firmly, but be prepared to listen to him. If he feels too tired (as opposed to bored) to cover the same distance again, don't ask him to do it. A tough, hilly or boggy 20 miles in bad weather can be much harder than a flat, easy 30 miles in good weather, and your first 40 miles should be as pleasant an experience as possible.

Taking your time

A horse who is 40-mile fit has started true endurance work, and your job is a question of keeping him ticking over at home but using competitions to test and improve his overall fitness or to increase the mileage and speed that you can both cope with. You are likely to find that your horse's speed will increase with maturity and as he develops a taste for work. As with increases in distance, horses often don't show what they are capable of in terms of speed until two or three seasons have elapsed. Initially it will take you around four or five months to have a previously unfit horse at 40-mile level; a mature horse who is already reasonably fit may be able to attempt a 40-miler within a couple of months.

I have had an already fit ten-year-old complete a 20, 30 and 40 within two months, and an eight-year-old novice complete two 25-milers then a 40 within three months. Your judgement is paramount and you should never over-stress your horse – if you do, you will face problems afterwards! Always err on the side of caution.

After your first season, you will have a much better idea of your horse's level of fitness and attitude, and your own capabilities. A mature, fit endurance horse is likely to come up to fitness again very quickly and may be able to start the season with a steady 40-mile ride. There is really little need to increase your work at home; just keep him ticking over.

Lungeing

In order to maintain or increase fitness, I like to lunge one day a week instead of riding. Lungeing is such a valuable substitute and can allow your horse to sustain a more constant pace than he would do out training. A fit horse can work on a lunge, just in a headcollar or cavesson with side-reins, for 30 or 40 minutes at a steady pace, provided that you use as wide a circle as possible – or, since circling can be quite punishing on the joints, lunge him instead on a large oval shape and move off centre yourself to accommodate his turns.

Lungeing provides a break from having you constantly on his back and riding the same old routes, as well as saving time. It is, however, more

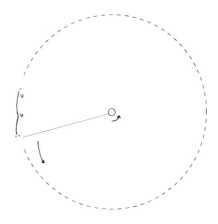

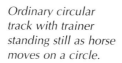

Ordinary circular track with trainer standing still as horse moves on a circle.

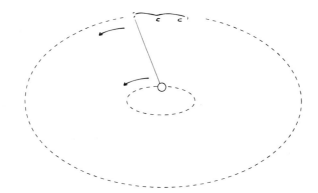

When lungeing for a prolonged period or at speed, make the area as wide as possible as if the horse is working in a school, and walk on an inside track parallel to his to allow him as much freedom of movement as possible.

strenuous on the legs, so carefully monitor what your horse is doing and don't give him the opportunity to throw himself around.

Some very fit endurance horses may be lunged and ridden during the same day or work session. I have only found it necessary to do this with horses of a less than laid-back character who have needed some of the edge taking off them before being ridden. Occasionally this happens with a fit horse who feels so well he's almost explosive!

Fast work

Once your horse is fit enough to start working at faster speeds for short periods of time, include some short fast rides as part of your weekly routine, as well as a few short canters during a long ride. Fast work is largely unnecessary for the earliest levels of endurance training, but once your horse is fit and you want to increase your speeds slightly, it can be very helpful. It should only be employed as a progressive means of fittening your horse once his system has already been fairly well conditioned. Any speed training can be a useful aid to enabling your horse to work at a

faster pace for rides with higher speed limits, races, or to help to produce the odd short sprint as and when necessary.

The aim of any fast work is to increase the efficiency of fast-twitch muscles. The two sub-divisions of fast-twitch fibre are high and low oxidative; high oxidative fibre works aerobically and will power a horse for work at a higher speed for a longer distance than slow-twitch muscle. However, in a horse who is unaccustomed to using fast-twitch muscle, low oxidative fibres abound. These produce powerful acceleration, but tire quickly and work anaerobically, using more glycogen and producing lactic acid, which can seriously impede a horse's performance as it builds up. Fast work therefore aims to condition the low oxidative fibre and adapt it to use oxygen, staving off the production of lactic acid during work. The overall effect is to condition the system to work at increasingly higher pulse rates and therefore raise the threshold of anaerobic work in practice.

Work to condition fast-twitch muscle is generally carried out in the form of interval training, according to a timed regime of gallop and recovery. There are various methods; the general method, following a warm-up ride, is to gallop a mile three times with a pulse recovery below 120 each time. Alternatively, gallop for 2 minutes with 3 minutes' walking recovery. The time between gallops allowed for recovery can be decreased as rates improve, and the gallop periods increased slightly. During your walk and before the next gallop, the pulse will usually fall to between 70-90bpm. If you don't have a pulse monitor or stethoscope,

Finishing in style! A horse in racing fitness prepared and able to give her all, even to the very last stride.

you will know when your horse has been working anaerobically if he slows down and is breathing deeply; he will be trying to replenish the oxygen in his system. In practice you can do the same job during a long ride at home, provided that your terrain is good enough to allow such fast work.

Rides to improve fitness

Once your horse has reached hard 50-mile fitness, you will be able to use rides themselves as a way of getting him fitter rather than doing much more work at home. Difficult or demanding rides with hilly terrain go a long way to improving a horse's fitness and any increase in mileage that your horse covers raises his fitness a notch or two. Listen to your horse and if he feels tired, pull out. It is always better to have a tired horse who didn't quite make the distance than an unsound one who completed. You need to be able to distinguish between tiredness and boredom, as horses can quickly get fed up and it's quite worrying if you aren't used to it! There is no need to overwork between rides and, providing you are careful about resting and working around and between competition, you should be able to improve his fitness slowly and keep upping the mileage gradually during the year.

Working around competitions

Maintenance of a fitness level throughout the season is not difficult, but learning to pitch your work so as not to overwork or tire your horse can be difficult for less experienced riders. The last few days before a ride his

---

1 *Up to 20/30 miles below 8mph (every 3 weeks)*

Mon   1 hour slow hack (6-7 miles)
Tue   Rest
Wed   1 hour steady schooling or lesson or gentle jumping
Thur $1^1/_2$ hours hack at steady trot (7mph) to cover up to 10 miles or up to 30 minutes lunge at steady trot or 30 minutes schooling and 1 hour hack
Fri   Rest
Sat   2 hours training ride up to 15 miles, at 7mph to include some steady cantering
Sun $1^1/_2$ hours training ride up to 12 miles, at 6mph to include one or two slightly faster canters

If your horse is working at this level he will easily cope with 20 miles at $7^1/_2$mph and 30 miles at 7mph.

Sample fitness programme in preparation for 20/30-mile rides.

2 *40 up to 60 miles at 8mph (once a month maximum)*

Mon 2 hours slow hack up to 9 miles at 6$\frac{1}{2}$-7mph, to include 30 minutes schooling
Tue Rest
Wed 1 hour steady schooling or lesson or jumping
Thur 2 hours hack at 7mph to include long, steady trotting or up to 40 minutes lunge at trot and canter
Fri Rest
Sat 2$\frac{1}{2}$ hours training ride at 7mph, up to 16-17 miles (can include 40 minutes schooling), to include long, steady trotting and cantering
Sun 2$\frac{1}{2}$-3 hours training ride at 7mph, up to 16-17 miles, to include 30 minutes schooling, and when fit once a week interval training

This level will prepare your horse easily for 40 miles at 8mph and over, or 60 miles at up to 8mph, or possibly longer rides at slower speeds. Once fit, cut back on Saturday's and Sunday's distance, to a maximum of 2 hours with a longer ride once a fortnight.

3 *Over 60 miles, racing, higher speeds and up to 100 miles*

Mon 1 hour slow hack (6-7 miles)
Tue Rest
Wed 1 hours schooling or lesson or jumping
Thur 1$\frac{1}{2}$ hours hack at 8mph to include one interval training session or several long, steady canters
Fri Rest
Sat 2 hours work at 7mph, up to 10 miles if hacking, to include 30 minutes schooling, or 40 minutes lunge at trot and canter, lots of steady trotting
Sun 2 hours hack at 8mph, up to 16 miles to include, if necessary, one interval session or several long, steady canters

At this stage you may need to cut back the work your horse does at home. Once he is fit he should not be overworked, just kept ticking over and saved for competitions.

Sample fitness programmes in preparation for rides of 40 miles and above.

work should be slightly lighter in order to leave some mental energy and plenty of glycogen in his system for use during a ride. It is a mistake to rest, though, which will only cause problems with feeding.

I like to give a horse around three days to recover from a ride of up to

50 miles, and for 60 miles and over about a week; 100-mile rides usually see the horse having several weeks' holiday in lieu!

Fitness for life

Every step of the way, keep the emphasis on education and enjoyment of your horse, getting to know how to manage him, and enjoying yourselves out on the trail. How you progress depends largely upon his age. I would not take a horse under five years of age to a ride at all, apart from plodding round local sponsored routes of low mileage – most societies don't allow five-year-olds to attend anyway. With a five-year-old, I would do a maximum of four or five rides in one season, and nothing over 25 miles. A six-year-old should be able to cope with 30 miles and a slow, flat 40-miler late in the season. A seven-year-old may be mature enough to complete a 50- or 60-miler or two, and at eight the speed and mileage can be increased. There are horses which are asked to do 100 miles in a day at seven years of age, or to race, but personally I don't feel that a horse is mature enough to cope with tough terrain, faster speeds or longer distances until he is at least eight or nine.

An endurance horse starts to mature at nine years of age and peaks between ten and fifteen, so there is no point in trying to rush a youngster. Bearing in mind that your horse has his whole life ahead of him, it is hardly worth pushing him too far and too fast in one ride; you need a horse left for the next ride! Endurance horses often go on competing into their late teens and early twenties. If you are starting out with a nine-year-old or older, that has been fairly fit before, you may be easily able to manage a 50-miler late in your first season, and go on to 60-plus the following year at fairly good speeds. It will usually take three seasons for a horse to reach a suitable level of physical fitness and mental tenacity to attempt a 100-miler or race at high speeds.

5

Feeding for Performance

Any athlete requires fuel with which to power the body. Due to the sustained nature of the work which you ask your endurance horse to do, he needs to receive a supply of energy that is easily metabolised and can be readily called upon to fuel the work that he does. There are a vast number of feeds available and ways to provide energy for your horse. However, with a system as finely tuned as the endurance horse's, and bearing in mind the amount of energy that you are going to ask him to use, you have to give him the best possible chance of receiving the right balance in his diet.

Basic diet

At rest or in light work only, the horse's requirements are relatively minimal. As the horse is naturally a foraging and grazing animal, his system has evolved to cope with this kind of diet. Therefore, the basis of his diet must be formed through feeding what he would naturally choose to eat himself. To fulfil this need, he should be turned out on good pasture for as much of the day as is possible or practical, or allowed to live out twenty-four hours and forage for himself.

Forage quality

The quality of your pasture must be taken into account as part of his daily diet, and should be managed according to the quality of forage you wish your horse to receive. Many soils are naturally deficient in certain minerals or have been leached of their content through years of farming or lack of maintenance. Any deficiencies in soil will result in pasture deficient in those same minerals, whether it be in the form of the grazing your horse is turned out on, or the hay he eats. If you are in any doubt, have your vegetation analysed and make up for any major deficiencies through additions elsewhere in the diet, and buy in hay from different sources to minimise the effect of deficiencies.

The quality of your horse's forage must be taken into consideration – in this case, a little too lush for a working diet. This podgy pony went on to become a regular and successful 50-mile endurance competitor.

Weeds which are harmful should be eliminated, and there should be as wide a variety of natural herbs and meadow plants as possible to provide your horse with some variation in his diet. It should be remembered that plants provide the horse's diet with various vitamins and minerals, and many have their own beneficial qualities. A horse allowed free access to choose what he eats will naturally fulfil his own cravings, but it is your responsibility to monitor his diet carefully as horses are unable to discern the nutritional value of the plants that they eat!

Extra needs

Whilst a purely natural diet will suffice for the horse in his natural environment, for maintenance and for light work, the horse subject to an increased workload will need a proportion of his diet to be supplemented with more energy, protein and mineral-dense foods. Fibre should still form around 75% of the diet of the competing horse. The additional nutrients will be provided by the remainder of his feed ration.

In order to understand his requirements, we first need to examine the way in which his system functions. Hard work requires an enormous amount of muscular activity. The fuel for muscular activity comes either from glucose in the blood, or from glycogen (a medium for storing glucose) in the liver and muscles. Glycogen in the muscles is metabolised to release energy through a chemical reaction caused by enzymes, which are also stored in the muscle cells. To fuel the entire process, oxygen is required.

Whether glucose or glycogen is used to fuel work depends upon the level of glucose present in the blood. The primary organ concerned with the maintenance of blood glucose levels is the pancreas, and it is therefore important for competitive riders to understand its function. The pancreas secretes both digestive juices and hormones. The hormones concerned are (1) glucagon, which encourages the breakdown of glycogen, raising the blood glucose level: and (2) insulin, which promotes uptake of glucose in the cells and inhibits breakdown of glycogen. Release of both hormones is controlled by blood-plasma glucose concentration. High levels of glucose in the plasma trigger secretion of insulin, causing cells to increase their glucose uptake and convert glucose into glycogen and fat for storage, thus decreasing the amount of circulating glucose. Low levels of glucose in the plasma trigger secretion of glucagon, causing cells to use less glucose for cell respiration and convert glycogen into glucose for use, thus increasing levels of circulating glucose.

Providing the fuel

Dietary energy for horses is usually expressed in terms of megajoules (MJ) of digestible energy (DE). Your horse's requirement for digestible energy can be calculated, based on his maintenance requirement and the additional energy needed for exercise. The average 500kg horse in moderate to heavy work requires between 100 and 140 MJ/DE per day. This sounds as though your horse will need to consume vast quantities of feed! However, feeding more than 2.25kg (5lbs) of concentrate feed at a time results in the stomach overflowing and pushing the feed into the small intestine. In turn, this results in incomplete digestion which can alter the gut pH and cause metabolic problems. An endurance horse therefore needs to be fed little and often, ideally two or three small meals a day. He also needs a high carbohydrate diet in order to supply the MJ/DE that is needed to work. During a long ride, a horse can't eat enough to fuel the work, so he must have a reserve to work on, which is the glycogen stored in his body. The better your feeding regime, the less glycogen will be lost from his muscles and liver.

The question, then, is how to provide readily available, long-lasting energy for your endurance horse. One main energy source is carbohydrate. Carbohydrates are metabolised at different rates – the most instantly available is glucose, followed by starch. These are easily digested and provide readily available energy. Unruly behaviour often occurs in horses as a result of too much glucose in the blood, resulting in an explosive feeling. Glucose is, however, essential for the nervous system, so is an imperative part of the diet.

For sustained energy, your feeding system should therefore contain some ingredients that are quickly metabolised and release energy instantly, and others that are metabolised more slowly to give an energy source over a longer period of time. Carbohydrates from fibre are metabolised more slowly than glucose and starch, and fats release energy more slowly than carbohydrate. They also contain 2.5 times more energy than carbohydrates if fed on a weight for weight basis, so that you can provide the necessary energy for your horse without adding to the bulk he has to consume. Feeding fat can also increase blood glucose levels by up to 50%. During work, this is used first and the body's stores of glycogen are spared, deferring fatigue. Therefore, the best way to maintain constant energy levels is on a high roughage, high fat diet – some French endurance horses are reputed to compete on high quality hay and oil alone! Grape seed and corn oil are currently thought to be the most effective as they contain high levels of linoleic acid (a fatty acid).

High-oil diets

When feeding a high-oil diet, however, several primary points have to be borne in mind. The first is that when feeding high levels of oil you should increase the vitamin E in the diet. Vitamin E is an anti-oxidant. When oil is digested, peroxides (free radicals) are formed as a by-product. These need to be oxidised before they cause harm to the horse. Vitamin E 'mops up' the free radicals. Selenium works in conjunction with vitamin E and most supplements will contain both vitamin E and selenium. Because of the fine balance between providing energy and upsetting the metabolism, therefore, it is also important not to feed more than 5% of the total diet as fat.

It is easy to see that feeding a competition horse is an art form as well as a science! There is a fine line between providing adequate fuel for work without depleting the system, and overloading the horse's metabolic function. The guiding considerations to bear in mind are that you should only increase the energy you feed to your horse after the workload has increased; that new ingredients must be introduced gradually; that feeds must be given little and often; and that on rest days, including the night before a rest day, the concentrate ration must be cut right down.

Azoturia

Azoturia normally affects fit horses on return to work after rest, although it may also be caused by over-working an unfit horse. Giving too much feed for the work the horse is doing will lead to increased storage of glycogen in the muscles. If the horse is rested and overfed, or exercised irregularly, glycogen will surge into the system when the horse next works. When rapid glycogen release occurs, not enough oxygen can be taken in to metabolise it. This results in the sudden build up of lactic acid in the muscles and azoturia occurs.

As the condition occurs whilst the horse is working, it is important to recognise the symptoms. The horse will have difficulty in moving forward, and the muscles, particularly in the hindquarters, will cramp and become solid. In severe cases, the horse may try to lie down as it becomes painful to stand, will pant to try and reduce the oxygen debt, and is likely to sweat. His urine will be dark brown and smell tangy, due to the breakdown of muscle fibres and release of myoglobin, which is being excreted.

The first thing to do is dismount, and keep the horse as warm and still as possible. Cover the hindquarters with your coat, or anything else you have with you that will help to insulate. Ideally you should be boxed home to prevent the risk of further muscle damage, although in very mild cases the horse may recover quickly enough to be walked gently home in hand. Call the vet immediately, who will administer a muscle relaxant, anti-inflammatory drug, and/or pain-killers. Following treatment, blood-testing is vital to determine the level of muscle damage that has taken place. Rest is paramount as working the horse too soon may cause a repeat attack, and his concentrate feed should be cut down, or removed until your vet advises you otherwise.

Electrolytes

Another cause of azoturia is an imbalance of salts, which causes difficulties in muscle metabolism. These salts should be included in the endurance horse's diet and replaced if lost through sweating. All of us think of losing 'salt' as we sweat, and as the endurance horse does a lot of sweating, he loses a great deal of 'salt'. What is lost is, in fact, a mixture of salt (sodium chloride) as well as other minerals, collectively

Administering electrolytes: these essential supplements are a must for endurance horses, but they don't always taste too good.

known as electrolytes, including calcium and potassium chloride. Hard work therefore increases the requirement for these ingredients in the diet.

These salts must all be replaced through use of an electrolyte in the diet at home and through supplementation on a ride. Salt should always be readily available, ideally in a stable lick or a block provided in the field, or as plain salt added to the feed. Electrolytes should never be given to the dehydrated horse, as the increase of salt in the gut will actually draw in water from the blood in an attempt to metabolise it, thus making the horse more dehydrated. If offered both during training and in the course of a ride, the horse will tend to naturally drink what he needs. In cases of horses who dislike the taste, however, syringes of electrolyte paste are used. These should always be administered while the horse is still fully hydrated, to prevent his system from becoming depleted of essential minerals.

Water

Even though this is an international race ride, every rider takes the opportunity to offer their horse water from this river on the route.

Water is also lost in sweat, and the endurance horse must always be kept fully hydrated in order to be able to function fully and perform to the best of his ability. The main organs involved in fluid level regulation are the kidneys. The kidneys metabolise waste products for excretion via

urine. If the horse receives more protein in the diet than he needs, then the excess nitrogen is removed via the urine, so a strong smell of ammonia may be indicative of a high protein level in the diet. Urine quality is therefore a valuable gauge to your horse's health. Apart from removing toxins from the blood in this way, the kidneys are effectively the body's filter system as they reabsorb the correct balance of salts and fluid, helping to maintain a constant mineral balance, pH and fluid level within the blood (homeostasis).

Adequate hydration at all times means keeping water in the system, and particularly in the gut, whilst at the same time preventing bloating and keeping the horse's weight at a reasonable level. One of the best ways to keep an adequate level of water in the gut is to feed a good proportion of fibre in the diet, and in this respect sugar-beet is an important ingredient in the majority of endurance horse's rations. Apart from being fed wet, sugar-beet contains high levels of pectin, a protein which absorbs water. Sugar-beet also contains highly digestible fibre and sugar and is extremely palatable. It is ideal for feeding during a ride and is a useful energy source for the endurance horse.

Blood

Blood plays a vital role in the balance of fluids within the body, particularly when the horse is sweating heavily. Blood tests can therefore be useful in monitoring your horse's health and provide a gauge of the correct functioning of the organs and level of fitness of the horse. Useful not only when problems occur (such as azoturia), blood testing can provide information on anaemia, bacterial infection, dehydration, red blood cell count (and effectively fitness level), kidney function, liver damage, muscle damage, viral infection and parasitic damage. Blood tests for information at home are generally taken when the horse is at rest and relaxed, although they are also taken during international competitive rides to test for doping.

Protein

Protein is required for growth, for production of enzymes and hormones, and for repair and maintenance of muscles. Protein is the least available source of energy to the horse. The use of protein as an energy source for horses can cause various metabolic problems and produce excess heat, which is a handicap to the endurance horse as it increases sweat production.

A mature horse needs 100g of protein in every kilogram of feed he eats. Be aware of the protein content of the forage your horse is eating; grass, hay and haylage will vary in their protein content and can sometimes provide all the protein that the horse needs. Although haylage actually contains less protein than hay on an as fed basis, it is more available to the horse. Haylage contains 50% more water than hay, so if you feed the same amount, weight for weight as you would hay, you will actually be decreasing the overall protein and fibre levels that your horse receives. It is therefore important to follow the guidelines on the haylage bales for feeding by weight and adjust your concentrate ration accordingly.

Other factors

B vitamins are important in energy cycles. They are manufactured courtesy of bacteria in the hind gut through the digestion of roughage. If enough roughage cannot be fed, vitamin B levels may need supplementing. Similarly, if the balance of bacteria in the hind gut is disturbed, for example by the chemicals involved in worming or through increased stress levels, the addition of a probiotic supplement may bring about an increase in condition and performance. Probiotics contain bacteria naturally present in the hind gut and supplement existing levels. Feeding a probiotic can bring about quite startling improvements in the horse's condition, particularly in a slightly poor horse or one who is naturally lean.

Hard work increases the level of stress through the horse's joints, and some believe that it may actually deplete the synovial fluid, or joint lubricating oil. The substances manufactured within the body to produce synovial fluid are in part chondroitin sulphates, and today supplements are available to top up the levels. These are said to have the effect of thickening the synovial fluid and cushioning the joint. Many riders find that the net effect to the horse is a smoother, freer action. Needless to say, this can make a huge difference to horses in hard work and at the end of a long ride the horse will benefit from being able to work more freely.

Putting it all together

We have examined the various components necessary to the endurance horse's diet. To summarise, these are carbohydrate, water, protein, vitamins and minerals, which are obtained from fibre and cereals. Looking at each group more specifically, we now need to formulate a diet for your horse. Assuming that fresh, clean water is constantly available to him, the next most basic ingredient in his diet is forage in the form of hay and pasture, which should be of as high a quality as possible. Hay and pasture analysis will help you to determine if any particular minerals or trace elements need supplementation. His short ration is likely to be based on sugar-beet, which contains both fibre and carbohydrate. Added to this, he must have protein and some form of supplementation,

A well-prepared
horse in good
condition – the
result of careful
attention to diet.

encompassing electrolytes, oil, minerals and vitamins, unless you feed a compound feed which will provide all he needs. Don't neglect any specific extras that he as an individual needs, such as biotin for increased hoof growth, a probiotic, etc.

At lower levels of work you may be well able to compete with a horse on sugar-beet, barley, a splash of oil and a basic vitamin and mineral supplement, or sugar-beet, oil and a compound feed which is fully supplemented. If you are doing rides of 30 miles and above, his energy requirements will increase and, rather than risk getting it wrong with straight feeds, it is worth using a specifically formulated performance feed added to your sugar-beet. Compound feeds are very successfully fed by great numbers of endurance riders in the UK and performance levels can be drastically improved when using this type of mix, than when using straight feeds of varying quality that may need multitudinous supplementation.

It is important when formulating a diet for a horse in hard work to employ the use of a nutritionist, who will be best able to advise you as to quantities and types of feed for your horse, their content, as well as necessary and safe supplementation. With the advent of so many companies producing feeds geared towards hard work and often with a high oil content, it is worth taking the time to find someone who will help you to formulate a diet for your horse, preferably by coming out to see him first.

You will notice that throughout this chapter I have avoided giving specific weights of ingredients for a competing horse's diet. This is purely because every horse is so individual that his feeding will be unique. There is no hard-and-fast 'miles per gallon' figure and even horses of similar sexes and weights will function differently according to their own metabolism, age, level of fitness, rider's weight and fitness, work programme, genetic disposition and daily management. However, all horses do have minimum energy requirements for specific workloads.

In practice

Once your horse's diet is formulated and working, it is up to you to adjust it around his workload and condition. In ordinary training his work and feed level should remain fairly routine, with a reduction the night before a rest day and on the rest day itself. Where a ride is concerned, feeding regimes are simply an extension of the same principle. Up to several days before a ride, your horse may be working quite hard, but it is advisable to slightly reduce the level of his work for two or three days prior to the ride, to allow his muscles and liver to build up stores of glycogen. His hard feed should correspondingly be slightly reduced. When travelling to a ride the day before, he is likely to need a reduction in hard feed as you may only be able to lunge him or take him for a gentle hack when you arrive at your stabling. On ride mornings, he should have a normal work-day breakfast, with the addition perhaps of a specifically formulated carbohydrate boost (see opposite), which will give an instant extra for him to work from. Always ensure that throughout the whole process he has free access to hay and, if possible, grazing.

In order to feed around a workload which fluctuates, you have to develop a good idea of how your horse functions, how he does on different types of food, how well his weight stays on and how much energy he has generally. The last thing you want to do is overfeed, risking metabolic problems and putting too much weight on a horse which he will have to carry. The more weight carried, the more energy he needs to use to carry it! However, an endurance horse should always have a little fat in reserve otherwise he will have nothing to work on and will either 'hit a wall' or lose too much weight during the course of a ride.

During a ride

During rides up to 20 and 30 miles, he is unlikely to need feeding, but should be regularly allowed access to water and, if he sweats, electrolytes. For mileages over this distance he will require regular energy top-ups, ideally in the form of whatever he likes best that is easy to digest and provides readily available energy. A typical on-the-hoof meal might include sugar-beet with oil, electrolyte and carbohydrate boost added, whenever you meet your crew. At longer halts or vet stops, once through the vet he should be offered hay as well and some of his regular grain or compound feed added to the sugar-beet, as well as plenty of succulents. It is inadvisable to feed before vetting – in a race you won't have time, but digestion raises the pulse rate which, for any ride, is an inadvisable risk to take.

Remember that you do not want to overload his system as his energy must be directed to work, and not to digesting his feed. Today, there are lots of carbohydrate-boost products including long-chain glucose polymers which can be syringed down your horse's throat to give a quick energy boost before, during and after a ride and which, judiciously used, can actually prevent your horse from that feeling of running out of petrol and aid a speedy recovery. Gone are the days when horses always 'hit a wall' at 30 or 40 miles – this feeling is simply due to a lack of available glycogen stores or glucose in the system, as well as possibly a build-up of lactic acid. With good preparation, careful riding and prudent management during the ride, this point should not be reached. The key is to find out what works for your horse and not to be afraid to try new systems or ideas.

After a ride

Following a ride, his system will be tired, and his meals should be small. If your regime in preparation and management throughout the ride has been good, he should recover quickly, and should not lose too much of his glycogen reserve or his body weight. Although horses on a long ride do lose weight, this should be quickly replenished. A final point to be borne in mind – on ride mornings, especially if you have stabled at a venue, your horse may be too nervous to eat his breakfast. Don't panic! Experience will teach him that he needs every morsel he can get and, during or after a ride when he has begun to relax, he will resume his normal eating habits. Just make sure that you offer him tempting, high-energy, well-balanced feeds in small quantities as often as possible and, if your preparation has been correct, you will not have a problem.

Sample diets

---

1 *15.1hh, 10-year-old Arab gelding doing 40-50 mile rides every few weeks*

2.25kg/5lbs competition mix
1.5kg/3$\frac{1}{2}$lbs soaked sugar-beet
5.5kg/12lbs meadow hay (or as much as the horse will eat)
200ml/7fl oz oil balanced for vitamin E & selenium

The above is split into two feeds, with an electrolyte supplement added in the evening. This horse is turned out daily for as long as possible.

---

2 *15.3hh, 7-year-old TB/Arab/Native cross mare, competing at 60 miles plus once a month, and aiming at 100 miles this season*

3.5kg/8lbs compound performance cubes
1.75kg/4lbs short-chopped alfalfa
1kg/2lbs soaked sugar-beet
4.5kg/10lbs hay (or as much as the horse will eat)

The above is split into three feeds with added electrolytes and garlic (a herbal supplement which many riders believe to be beneficial to health), with the hay given separately at night. This horse is turned out daily for as long as possible.

---

3 *14.3hh, 12-year-old Arab/Native pony cross, doing 20-40 mile rides all season*

1kg/2lbs micronised barley
1kg/2lbs soaked sugar-beet
chaff
3.5kg/8lbs hay
Plus broad-range vitamin and mineral performance supplement

The above is split into two feeds with a palmful of salt added to each feed along with a hoof growth supplement. This pony is turned out daily for as long as possible but his hay ration is restricted to keep his weight down.

6

Equipment

Endurance riding involves long hours for your horse under saddle and, for you, in it. Therefore everything that you use must be selected to cause the minimum physical stress to both you and your horse. The slightest irritation can, with repeated movement and over a prolonged period of time, cause extreme discomfort and affect both your horse's performance and your own.

During a ride of over 30 miles, you are likely to have to remove your tack at least once for vetting. The horse's sweating, weather and riding conditions will also mean that you need to change various items of tack at regular intervals during a long ride. Everything you use must therefore be lightweight, comfortable in the extreme, simple to use and care for and ideally, very tough and durable. It sounds a lot to ask, and it is.

Saddle design

If starting out with a novice horse, as long as your tack fits and is comfortable and easy for both of you to use, there is no reason at all why you should not compete with a general-purpose saddle, girth, saddle pad and ordinary bridle. The design of many GP saddles is improving and as long as yours is wide enough at the front to allow your horse freedom of movement, is well cut and fits correctly then there is no reason why you shouldn't continue to use it.

Where the endurance horse is concerned, saddle fit is perhaps more important than in any other equine discipline because of the sheer amount of time that you spend on the horse's back, both in training and during competition. The main factor to bear in mind with regard to the horse's comfort is that you are asking him to carry the burden of your weight. It is absolutely vital that his saddle fits and allows him to function fully; if not, the result will be physical problems and behavioural difficulties.

For all of these reasons, several design features are advisable. Firstly, the tree must be wide enough to accommodate his musculature and action. Many endurance horses may have a lot of shoulder action due to having a long stride, and the saddle must accommodate this and not pinch at every step. Saddles are often placed too far forward up the horse's wither, which encourages pinching, so check that yours is sited far enough back and is of the right length to allow the full range of movement both in front and behind.

The arch and gullet must be wide enough to avoid his spine, with as much clearance as possible; many saddles are still cut with narrow gullets that only just miss the vertebrae either side and that taper towards the back, which the horse's spine does not. The panels must be wide enough to distribute your weight as far across your horse's back as possible, and not concentrate it all in one area, creating excessive pressure and possible tissue and muscle damage; panels of the correct design will also encourage him to move as easily and freely as possible. The saddle must be balanced both laterally and medially; that is, it must not rock from side to side or front to back, or tip up or down either way. Any imbalance causes excess pressure on the flat, but the problem is exacerbated on hilly or rough terrain.

The seat should ideally be fairly flat and not place the rider at the back of the saddle in a little hollow, but allow you to sit centrally and upright without having to struggle against the design of the tree. Ideally, stirrup bars should not be so recessed that they necessitate a narrow tree, but should not sit out under your thighs. As far as I am aware no saddle has yet been manufactured with the stirrup bars in a central, comfortable position, partly due to limitations of design, but you should look for them being as close to beneath you as possible.

The flaps should be fairly straight to allow you to ride reasonably long, preferably without too much blocking or big rolls, but with just a little knee and/or thigh block to jam your leg against in times of trouble. Girth straps need to be easily reached and manipulated from the saddle.

Because of the demands upon design, many types of saddle are largely unsuitable for endurance. Most saddles would be uncomfortable for horse and rider for long periods of sustained riding. Jumping saddles are too forward cut and place the leg too close up to the rider's body for comfort, as well as tending to push the rider to the back of the saddle. Dressage saddles are generally too straight cut and concentrate the rider's weight into a small central area. Western saddles are sometimes seen, but are often too heavy and cumbersome for easy use. Working-hunter type saddles, surprisingly enough, often fulfil the criteria and can be ideal for endurance work, though you may need to add a 'seat-saver' for your own comfort.

GP saddles can be suitable but again, do make sure that yours allows your horse to work, does not hinder him or cause any discomfort, and allows you to ride fairly long and in a secure position. Once you have developed a longer leg position you are likely to find that a GP saddle tends to leave an awful lot of flap in front of your leg.

Any saddle which is heavy is a disadvantage unless you are extremely light and need to ride to weight. It will be difficult to lift on and off and is likely to add to the build-up of heat beneath the saddle. Anything with complex girthing arrangements can also cause problems, as you need to be able to adjust your girth fairly regularly when in the saddle.

Endurance saddles

There are currently three main types of endurance saddle: the GP based, the Western based, and the suspension or cavalry type system. All are designed to fulfil the criteria of comfort for horse and rider over long periods of time, but each type of design varies in the way it addresses the various issues of concern.

The GP-based designs start with a very GP-looking saddle that you can do other things with and that no-one would really notice was an endurance saddle, which is ideal if you compete in other disciplines. (Examples of these are Lovatt & Ricketts or Arlington saddles.) They are slightly straighter cut than a GP and have slightly extended panels, and possibly a slightly padded seat, with a few extra D-rings. However, they rarely go far enough in design to address the issue of weight-saving and distribution. Remember that a saddle that is cut short, with a short-backed horse in mind, needs to at least have panels which extend sideways; if the panels are not extended then the only thing about the saddle which is 'endurance' is the extra brass fittings!

A development of this design is the real 'English' type of endurance saddle such as the Pathfinder or Paragon, with a quilted or padded seat and lots of D's, fairly straight cut with a secure knee block and panels that extend to distribute the weight. These do the job really well and are comfortable and durable enough to last for many miles and many years. They are not, however, particularly lightweight, though are rarely too heavy to be easily handled. The use of a rigid or spring tree varies but some spring-tree saddles can tend to give a rather bouncy, banana-ish feeling and are not always conducive to correct riding.

The Western type of endurance saddle looks like a lighter, modified version of a Western saddle with less bulk and fancy extras, for example the Kidby. Based on the McClellan tree, which has a wide centre that allows for the horse's spine, these are cut straight without any blocking. They are available with padded seats, and the girth rigging allows for a greater range of adjustment than with the English style saddles. There is very little bulk between your leg and the horse, just one sweat flap, and the seat is very comfortable. However, the panels are not always extended to spread the rider's weight, and these saddles can be slightly heavy to lift.

The suspension system saddles (such as Orthoflex, Roe Richardson)

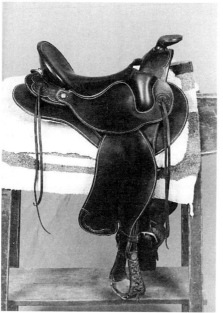

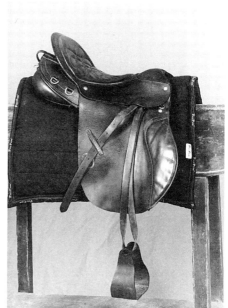

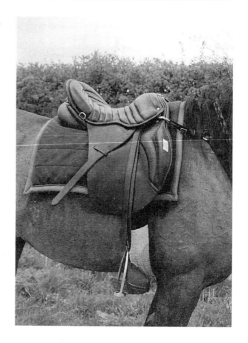

Above left: *Orthoflex saddle and Navaho-style woollen saddle blanket, with Western stirrups. This saddle has a suspension system.*

Above right: *Paragon saddle with Flex-Ride stirrups and PolyPad.*

Right: *A Pathfinder saddle, one of the English type of endurance saddles, with a padded seat, a fairly straight flap and extended panels to distribute the rider's weight.*

operate by actually absorbing the horse's motion before it reaches the rider. The panels are attached to the seat via pivot or suspension attachments, which cushion the rider from the horse – it feels a little like riding on a hovercraft. The panels are adjustable to the shape of each horse, which is a bonus as your horse changes shape. Seat design depends on the model of saddle but the endurance designs tend to be fairly flat and place the rider in a wonderfully secure, long riding position. Some designs have very little between your leg and the horse, which not only saves weight but goes a long way towards comfort for both horse and rider.

Bear in mind that your horse's weight and musculature will change as he gets fitter and that, as your saddle will often be wet and muddy, it is likely to need regular maintenance. There are no short cuts and it is imperative that either you have a good, forward-thinking saddler fairly locally who is prepared to come out and look at the saddle in action, or that you have a good after-sales service agreement with whomever you bought the saddle from. Today, some endurance saddles are approaching the price of horses, so invest carefully and be entirely sure that you are getting the right piece of equipment. Most endurance saddlers will either come out to see you or have a variety of saddles which you can try out.

It is worth saying a word here about synthetic saddles. As yet, leather is still proving to be far and away more suitable for endurance saddle manufacture, though advances are being made in the use and manufacture of various synthetic materials. Synthetic saddles are extremely light and easy to keep clean and handle. However, the materials have a habit of spreading during use, particularly the panels, which can mean that you end up with the tree pinching, especially at the front. These saddles are cheap to purchase and can be particularly useful as a standby or temporary measure.

Saddle pads

Again, there are three main types of saddle pad: the basic cloth, numnah or blanket; the padded or quilted type; and the gel- or foam-filled pad.

The designs of individual pads must number in their hundreds at the very least. The trick is to find what works for you, with your saddle on your horse. The main priority with anything that goes between your horse and his saddle is that it fits exactly, does not wrinkle and stays in place. It must have a good sweat uptake, allow the horse's skin to breathe, be easy to use and handle and stand up to the real hammering that constant use and washing put it through. The use of natural fibres such as cotton, wool and sheepskin seem to have the best properties as far as sweat absorption is concerned.

Plain numnahs and cloths should always be made of or covered with either cotton or wool. Thin cloths of this type are less than ideal for endurance as their design is rarely suitable for an endurance saddle. No matter how well cut, they tend to move, particularly over hilly terrain. They are also less able to absorb sweat and can be fiddly to fit and change during a ride if they have to be attached to the girth straps. Sheepskin numnahs are ideal, so long as they are cut to fit the saddle. Today many are treated to make them easier to wash and keep clean.

Lots of endurance riders use Navaho-style woollen saddle blankets, or any woollen blanket folded to fit. The trick here is to use something that doesn't need too many folds as it can become tricky to change. Blankets should also not cover too large an area of the horses's back, trapping heat and causing excessive and unnecessary sweating. Woollen blankets can absorb a great volume of sweat and are ideal for just turning over at a halt or vet gate.

Quilted or duvet-type pads, provided they are the right thickness, are excellent for the job. They generally have no attachments to get in the way, so you can turn them easily during the course of a ride, they absorb a great deal of sweat, stay in place and are covered with linen-type materials. They are light, simple and quick to change and wear very well during a long season and many spins in the washing machine. However, if too thin they can wrinkle, and if too thick can slip out or push the saddle too high up off the horse's back.

Gel-filled and foam-filled pads should not be necessary if your saddle fits correctly. However, as a very temporary measure to even out surface distribution, they can work wonders. The less bulky types have a role to play as an alternative to the duvet-style pads and help to cushion and absorb shock travelling through the horse's back.

All of the above comments tend to apply to seat-savers which, if your saddle doesn't have a padded seat or you don't, can help to cushion the strains.

Girths

The main issue with your girth is that it either absorbs sweat or works in harmony with it, that it is wide and comfortable, does not chafe or pinch and is easy to use. Again there are many types of girth available, the most basic of which are either leather or the padded fabric kind. Both should have an elastic end which allows the horse's barrel to expand. Leather girths work beautifully. The fabric type are easier to look after and less expensive, but do make sure that they have a high cotton content on the side against the horse. Any seams and joins on the girth should be nowhere near the horse's skin.

Incidentally, many saddles come with their own designs or types of girth. Endurance saddles that only have one sweat flap between your leg and the horse often work in conjunction with dressage-style girths, that are padded or covered all round with leather or another material to protect the horse's skin from buckles and stitching. One kind is covered in neoprene, which is an excellent material for use anywhere against horse's skin. It is lightweight and extremely tough, but it breathes and allows the horse to sweat freely through it, vastly reducing the occurrence of sweat rash. Sheepskin sleeves are also useful if your horse tends to suffer with flaky skin during and after a long ride. Woollen Western-style girths are an alternative that is sometimes used with these saddles. It is worth mentioning here that any of your horse's items should be washed with an absolute minimum of detergent. Anything soapy left in the fabric can irritate the skin and add to the problems with sweat rash.

Stirrups and leathers

Leathers should always be non-stretch and have a wide range of adjustment. They should be as wide and flat as possible to prevent chafing against your leg, although this is actually caused by a poor riding position rather than the equipment. You should be able to adjust your leathers easily when mounted as, during long periods, you may want to change your leg length slightly.

Old-style stirrup irons are rarely seen at an endurance ride. Today most riders prefer some form of caged front stirrup, enabling them to ride in footwear without a heel, and a wide tread, which helps to distribute the pressure on the foot. Western-style stirrups have a wide tread but, depending on the material from which they are manufactured, can be heavy and difficult to maintain, particularly if they are leather-covered. There are various stirrups manufactured of lightweight plastic polymer materials that flex and absorb the shock to the ankle and foot, making for a lighter, more comfortable ride. This can produce a significant reduction in fatigue and pain over a long ride. Flex-Ride stirrups also come with a shock-absorbing foot pad and in caged or open-toe options, and need no maintenance other than a quick dunk in a bucket when muddy.

Other leatherwork

Some saddles are recommended for use with breastplate or crupper attachments and, if your saddle is prone to moving over rough terrain or on steep hills, you will need them. Make sure they are well padded either with sheepskin or neoprene to minimise pressure and chafing and to absorb sweat. Breastplates should always be of the V-shaped hunter design rather than the flat breastgirth type seen on racehorses, which can restrict the horse's breathing if fitted too high. Martingales may also need to be padded or covered for the same reason, and standing martingales should never be attached to hackamores, as the action of both will be hampered.

Bridles and reins

Bridles need to be as simple and as comfortable as possible for a sweaty head that will regularly be doused with water. Catches and buckles need to be big enough to be operated with gloved hands, and straps need to be flat and light so as to minimise any pressure and sweating. Because of

Right: A washable Biothane bridle. The bridle bit unclips so that it converts to a headcollar.

Far right: A webbing combination endurance bridle, with hooks for easy bit removal and a loop at the back for a lead rope. These are easy to care for and are not affected by copious amounts of water.

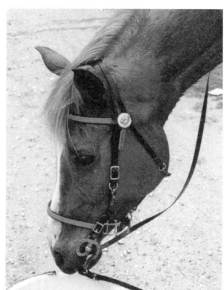

these requirements, synthetic materials are almost a must where bridles are concerned as they are light, comfortable, tough, have good-sized fittings and stand up to the numerous soakings. Best of all, the only maintenance they need is to be thrown in the washing machine or scrubbed in a bucket instead of all the fiddling about with soaping and cleaning tiny leather straps.

The most popular synthetic bridles are the convertibles, which have a clip on each side to enable you to take the horse's bit out within a matter of seconds, leaving a headcollar. This facility is excellent for allowing the horse to eat or drink at vet gates when he needs every moment to try and refuel, and saves messing about trying to unbridle an excitable horse. The beauty of this design is also in its sheer simplicity – you put it on by hooking up the throatlash, nothing more. Real time and trouble-saving pieces of equipment like these are absolutely invaluable. These bridles are currently made from two different materials: nylon webbing and plastic-coated webbing. Personally I favour the plain webbing ones as you can clean them in the washing machine.

Both types of convertible bridle come with their own reins, which can be plain or plaited. The plaited ones seem to offer the best grip, particularly when wet or sweaty. Horses, even laid-back endurance horses, often become extremely headstrong in packs or when there are other horses ahead, so do not underestimate the grip that you will need. The reins that offer the best purchase are the webbing type with little leather stops along them, which are just as easy to handle when wet as when dry. However, these are not particularly long and when your competing involves a combination of leaping on and off, riding, leading and handling from the ground, it can be useful to have slightly longer reins than you would normally use. Rubber-coated reins are not as favourable because they are thicker and give less feel with the mouth, and slip when wet. Plain reins tend not to offer much grip.

To bit or not to bit

Whatever braking and steering you use must be designed so as not to injure your horse's mouth. Keen, fit horses in the company of others generally behave far more strongly than at home and, if you are to stay in control and not risk exhausting your horse during the first 15 miles, you need an effective bitting arrangement. Although your horse will generally take between 7-15 miles to settle, you need to be able to teach him to control and conserve his energy, apart from emergency stopping and turning and directing him across bad going. Horses generally have a preference over whether they like to go bitless, with a jointed bit or a straight bar bit. Contrary to popular belief, the majority of horses, particularly those with soft mouths, do not go completely happily in a jointed bit.

Hackamores come in various designs according to the severity of their action; generally, the longer the shank, the stronger the action. Flat nosebands produce less pressure than rolled nosebands, and leather curb

A fit horse going fairly strongly in a German hackamore. Note the rider's riding tights and trainer boots for running.

straps are less severe than chains. Whatever combination you use, pad it all well, with sheepskin or neoprene, to prevent chafing or pressure bumps and to absorb sweat.

Horses with extremely soft mouths may go more happily in bitless bridles. Conversely, they provide extra control for very strong horses who have a tendency to lean on your hands. The curb action helps to keep the head in the right place, and of course having no bit eliminates the risk of bruising or chafing the mouth.

The worst bruising and chafing tends to occur with jointed bits that pull on the soft corners of the mouth, so it is worth putting Vaseline on the bit corners and the mouth to help the bit to slide against the skin rather than pulling on it. Straight bar bits with a little curb action, such as pelhams, the bradoon of a double bridle, or a Western curb with a leather strap are a good compromise. They produce enough flexion to keep the head at the right level, and don't bruise or pinch the mouth. For horses who get impossibly strong, gags are permitted, but must be used with two reins. Whatever tack you use, it must be safe, well maintained, fit correctly and be checked over regularly to minimise the possibility of breaking.

Leg protection

The rules of each society vary on the use of protection according to the distance and type of class you are entering, so do be sure to check before you go. The whole point of endurance riding is that the horse stays sound over the distance, and one point of view is that if the horse needs boots on to do it, he is not a really tough, sound horse. However, if you intend to use brushing, over-reach or tendon boots, they must fit perfectly and you must either change or clean them at regular intervals throughout the ride. If the boots trap any grit or collect a mud build-up, the result can be an injury – or even lameness if the action is impeded.

Rugs

As your horse is going to be 'parked' and rested for various periods before, during and after rides, you need to be well equipped with appropriate rugs and always with plenty of layers, whatever the weather. Even on a hot day horses can shiver if it suddenly rains or is windy, and during most rides there will be inclement weather of some kind. The heat built up in the muscles needs to escape gradually as the horse cools down, or he needs to be kept warm between sections and during halts. Rugs should therefore be light, possess insulation properties, whilst allowing heat and moisture to escape slowly. There are various fabrics and fillings and it is worth looking around at a ride to see what works; Flectalon is a very effective filling and insulates efficiently.

Too many fiddly straps are a nightmare when it comes to whipping rugs on quickly to keep a horse warm, and getting them off again fast for the vet. One strap in the front with easy-to-release fastenings (remember your gloved or cold fingers) and a couple of crossed surcingles underneath are ideal. Straps should be easy to alter for length, according to whether the horse is saddled or not. Always spend an extra couple of seconds to fasten a rug – all too often one sees horses panicking as their rugs slide off behind, risking injury to themselves, often causing it to their handlers, and inevitably raising the horse's pulse.

You may well need several layers in cold weather and often need to add or take layers out from one moment to the next. You will need to take a New Zealand or a rain sheet for bad weather, as well as a close-weave sweat rug, a couple of sweat sheets, or a sweat sheet and a light rug so that he can be kept warm while he cools down.

Pulse monitors

Many people will be happy managing with a stethoscope and this is fine, particularly if you know your horse well and ride him accordingly. However, for higher levels of fitness training, serious race riding or if your horse's pulse returns unreliable parameters, investment in a pulse monitor is truly worthwhile. Using one in training will help you to gain valuable knowledge about the rates at which your horse works in various paces, and how factors like weather, the terrain, and distractions affect him. In competition, you can literally ride with an eye on the clock, giving you an advantage when presenting for vet gates, and alerting you as soon as your horse shows signs of fatigue.

At present, affordable pulse monitors (or heart rate monitors, as they are also called) are still somewhat bulky, although research constantly improves design. There is also talk of adjusting cyclists' speedos for equine use, giving accurate read-outs of distance covered, speed and

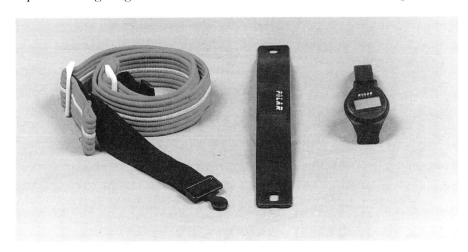

A wireless pulse monitor. In the centre is the transmitter, which is positioned over the pulse point using the strap on the left to keep it in place. The 'watch' is the receiver, showing the read-out.

heart rate. Whilst this type of instrument is a helpful safety net and reassurance as well as being educational, it has to be remembered that the horse is an animal, not a machine, and no amount of gadgets will make up for your ability to ride and manage him.

Rider equipment

The first thing to realise is that you do not actually need anything other than boots with a heel, jodhpurs, a regulation standard hat and a shirt. However, as you spend more time in the saddle you will begin to feel the need for more comfort and protection than these ordinary items can bring. Everything should fit, allow you to move, allow your body to breathe, insulate or keep you cool, and nothing should wrinkle, bag, pinch or rub.

Hats

To start with, there are many kinds of hat which meet the safety standards. Rules state that hats have to be to BSI or an equivalent or higher standard. The lighter your headgear, the more comfortable you will feel.

A professionally equipped pair. The horse wears a combination bridle, PolyPad and Flex-Ride stirrups. The rider is equipped with a Hatrick hat cover, half chaps, riding trainers and a waist bag for drinks and first-aid kit.

Lightweight, ventilated hats are the ultimate in comfort, and prevent the build up of heat and sweat which becomes so irritating during a long ride. If you use a silk over a crash cap, opting for a pale colour in hot weather will also help to keep your head cool. There are now some soft-top covers that you can add which shade and help to keep the wind and rain off your face and neck.

Footwear

The main features of endurance footwear are that it needs to absorb the shock as well as keep your feet cool, provide foot support and ideally have a good grippy sole for when you walk or run. Ideally, it should be relatively waterproof too, although having both waterproofing and breatheability is an impossibility where footwear is concerned. Many people ride in jodhpur or riding boots, but trainers provide much more cushioning; purpose-designed riding trainers and performance footwear are now starting to provide for our needs. Some prefer to wear half-chaps to protect the lower leg and provide some extra grip.

Jodhpurs

Traditional jodhpurs are still seen at rides but rarely, as the seams are in the worst place possible for long periods in the saddle. Whatever fabric is used, it also has a tendency to bag behind the knees and wrinkle at the top of the legs. Lycra riding tights with padding in the seat and knee and, if preferred, grippy suede knee patches have revolutionised riding wear for endurance riders. They are light, fit like a second skin, stretch to move with you, are durable, look good and dry out almost instantly. Better still, they enable you to ride in complete comfort without the need for underwear, which is the bane of any endurance rider's life. Neoprene or fleece jodhpurs are ideal for cold and wet weather use and protect you from the worst of the rain and cold, as well as fitting well and feeling extremely soft and comfortable.

Shirts

Shirts should be loose, and under BHS rules you must have a collar as opposed to riding in a vest or T-shirt, even in hot weather. Natural fabrics are definitely the order of the day as they keep your body warm in cool weather, cool in warm weather and allow your skin to breathe. Any top you wear needs to be long enough not to leave a chilly gap at the back when you move or lean forward, and a little extra length in the sleeves allows for reach. The collar should have a opening (placket) below it, so that you can leave a few buttons open to allow for comfortable movement of your neck.

Coats

It is always advisable to take at least one good coat with you to a ride – even if the weather looks set to scorch all day. Advanced manufacture of materials has led to a whole new breed of coats which are lightweight, comfortable, insulating, warm, windproof, waterproof and breatheable, minimal in bulk and cut to allow you to move and ride comfortably at all times. Pockets need to be easy to get at, and zips and fastenings must be chunky so that you can operate them by feel or with cold or gloved hands. These items are expensive, but will last for many seasons and, once you have had the benefit or a really warm, waterproof, windproof, comfortable coat during severe weather, you will realise why they are such a boon.

A well-equipped horse and rider. The horse has an Orthoflex saddle with neoprene-covered girth and a minimal bridle with a rubber pelham. The rider wears a ventilated Saratoga hat, cross-country top and riding tights.

Other kit

Padded underwear if you wear jodhpurs is a must, and for women, a really strong supportive sports bra which is comfortable and fits. Straps should be wide and soft so as not to cut in anywhere, even if you move suddenly.

You should always take gloves, in case your horse gets strong, for cold and wet weather as well as general protection. Neoprene is ideal, but make sure you go for those with suede or rubber-type grippy patches between the fingers, or you will end up losing your reins. Fleece materials are excellent in cold weather but, again, you need some grip. Sadly, very few gloves are made thin enough to give a good feel, warm enough for cold and wet weather, and with a grip. Leather is OK but does not stand up to the hammering that endurance work gives it, and is not particularly warm. The woollen or stretchy material gloves with rubber grip palms are fine and can be treated as a disposable commodity as they are so economical.

Socks should either be of a natural fibre, which perform beautifully but don't last very long, or an insulating ski-tube-type sock, or a walking sock with a padded sole. Unless your footwear lets moisture out and keeps warmth in, sweat and dampness are a problem, and on a long ride you may need a regular change of socks, particularly in wet weather.

A neckerchief or bandana is useful to have around your neck to put over your nose and mouth if it's very cold, wet or dusty. It also helps to prevent rain running down your neck and can act as an emergency bandage or tie.

Whips are a matter of personal choice but according to the rules must be under 30ins (76cms), around average riding crop size. Have one with a button top so that you don't drop it.

On a long ride or where crew access is difficult, it is a good idea to ride with a bum-bag or pouch around your waist – many riders prefer to do so anyway. Mine contains change for the telephone, a folding hoof-pick, baler twine, a whistle, a clean bandage, a sponge, a tiny pot of wound powder, the phone number for the ride venue, vet or farrier and one or two energy bars. You can put your gloves in if you take them off, too. During the course of a ride I never open my bag except to eat the energy bars, but it is advisable to have the bare minimum of emergency equipment. A compass is only useful if you know how to use one and have a map with you. Carefully packed, your pouch should weigh next to nothing and take up little space, and you never know when you may have an injury, accident or need to help someone else in the same situation.

It is advisable to carry fluid with you to drink, either in a bottle attached to the saddle or in the CamelBak fluid back-packs. These come in two sizes and can be refilled by your crew without you taking them off. The smaller size holds 0.75l (roughly a pint and a quarter), which lasts for around 20-25 miles if you sip constantly. Map cases are available from camping and walking shops and it is a good idea to have a copy of your route on the side you can see, with your times on the back and your checkpoint card, if you need to carry one.

Whatever the combination of riding tack and equipment for your horse and yourself, the minimalist approach is best. The less you have to take, put on, take off and handle, the less there is to worry about going wrong or losing.

7

Personal Preparation

Endurance riding is physically very demanding on you as a rider in the same way as it is on the horse. In the most basic terms, your horse will find himself unable to perform, no matter how well he is prepared, if you are a hindrance to him rather than an asset. As a rider, therefore, you must be well balanced and technically able at all times to help a tiring horse to cope with difficult terrain. In order to do this, you should be as fit and as well conditioned and prepared as your horse.

Fitness training for your horse involves development in the form of balance, suppleness and muscular strength as well as efficiency of cardiovascular and aerobic function. Your own personal preparation and training should involve the same key elements. However, your job as a rider does not end here. As well as being physically able to cope with the task in hand, your horse is relying on you to guide him over the correct course, pace him, keep him safe, make strategic and management decisions, and successfully present him to the vet. Therefore, you also need to be mentally prepared and organised for what you are going to do.

Fit to ride?

Riding produces a basic level of fitness in the rider just as it does in the horse. However, it is fair to say that unless you put some additional work into your own preparation, you may well tire more quickly than your horse. You are likely to have to dismount and walk or run with your horse over treacherous going, and riding as such will not prepare you for this. The bottom line is that the fitter you are to ride, the better you will be able to help your horse to do what you are asking him to do, instead of hindering him and reducing his level of performance. There is little point in devoting your entire energy into producing a fit, sound, well-conditioned, turbo-fuelled equine athlete who can do 50 miles without blinking, if you are exhausted at 30! Apart from helping your horse, you are effectively helping yourself. It can be extremely unpleasant to suffer the after-effects of a long ride when you are in unfit condition, and doing

You need to be as fit as your horse to compete in endurance riding, particularly when it comes to helping him through some really muddy terrain!

your utmost to eliminate the pains and strains actually makes the whole experience far more pleasant for you, as well as those around you.

Training beforehand will also help to conserve your horse's energy during the ride as you will be more able to maintain a balanced riding position. Just as you have schooled your horse for balance, suppleness and muscular strength, and trained him for increased efficiency of cardiovascular and aerobic function, your own preparation should follow the same principles. Before you make any attempt to get fit, you must first of all balance yourself. You would not try and get your horse fit if he was dragging himself along from the forehand or constantly cantering on one lead, as his muscular development would be uneven and his efficiency limited. In the same way, it is of little use to a rider to get fit if your overall performance is unbalanced.

A balancing act

Most people naturally favour one side of their bodies, just as they are right- or left-handed. You are probably just as right- or left-legged, with corresponding physical imbalances. Poor posture when seated and walking cannot suddenly be transformed into good posture in the saddle, so you must attempt to remain balanced throughout the rest of your routine, not just when riding. If, for example, you tend to cross your legs one way, you are automatically twisting your spine and collapsing the hip on the side of the supporting leg. Your weight when riding is very likely to be placed more on this seatbone. Habits such as these affect your balance and weight placement when riding, as well as your muscular development and, ultimately, that of your horse.

In an attempt to retrain your own body to move and work in a balanced way, various techniques are worth consideration. The Alexander technique teaches methods of physical awareness. By becoming more aware of how you use your own body, using visualisation and balancing exercises, you become more able to reposition yourself in a balanced way. Breathing is also an important part of this technique and it is important to learn how to breathe properly when undertaking any form of physical exercise. Most of the time, we only use the top part of our lungs and take short, frequent, incomplete breaths. However, learning to use your total lung capacity is a valuable aid to fitness training as well as for use in times of stress. Yoga is also helpful in focusing your attention upon the way you use your own body.

Riding technique

Balancing your own posture both in and out of the saddle can only assist your horse, and, as I mentioned in the chapter on schooling, it is well worth getting some advice or training on your riding – no matter how well you think you can ride. You only need to look at photographs of riders to spot some appalling riding faults. Largely the perpetrators are unaware of their errors – and no, none of us is exempt! World-class international riders down to novice weekend pleasure riders can all benefit from tuition. If you are in any doubt, the easiest way to convince yourself is to hire or borrow a video or camcorder and see for yourself! Ideally rope in a friend or crew member who also rides to assassinate the video afterwards, as it can be difficult to spot or be honest about your own failings.

Riding without reins and stirrups on the lunge can be invaluable in deepening your seat and eliminating postural problems but, just as you want to improve your horse's performance, you have to want to improve your own performance for headway to be made.

Riders who have had no tuition for many years are often delighted with the benefit they gain from a few flatwork lessons, ideally with their own horse; and it can be highly enlightening to feel the difference that slight adjustments in posture or technique can make to your horse's performance and your own. Granted, few endurance riders wish to ride an Advanced dressage test, but it is unfair to expect your horse to work in a balanced, rhythmic, efficient and co-ordinated way without your ability to allow him to do so. It is impossible to school your own horse for balance and suppleness if you don't possess the necessary know-how! Nowadays there are plenty of seminars and short courses for riders of

Horse and rider travelling at speed, the rider well balanced over the horse's centre of gravity.

every sphere, level of ability and interest which can enhance your riding and your horse's performance. Even problems which you might meet unexpectedly out on the trail, such as your horse hotting up in other's company, will be easier for you to deal with if you have the right skills. The worst thing for other riders to encounter out on a ride is a bad-mannered or unruly horse with a rider who is panicking, unable to control the beast or unsure of what to do!

Stretching exercises

Once you have made every effort to rebalance your posture and improve your technique, you need to be able to maintain these abilities and apply them in a riding situation. In order to do this you have to become supple and learn to move with your horse as he works. Suppleness comes from the development of muscles and their use and from training them to perform chosen functions. In particular, a supple back is extremely important for absorbing the horse's motion. It is pointless training yourself to peak fitness and becoming so musclebound that you cannot lift your leg as high as the stirrup or bend to adjust your girth from the saddle or to unfasten a gate! Therefore, instead of high impact, jerking, repetitive exercises which shorten and thicken muscles, you need to perform the same kind of work as your horse –

prolonged, slow, steady, gentle exercise.

Basic stretching exercises can be done slowly and gently in the comfort of your own home, and require no special equipment. Callanetics is a technique which concentrates on muscle development through slow but deeply effective stretching and suppling exercises, and is used successfully by riders the world over. The key is to keep exercises slow and gentle and to breathe properly throughout. Remember that no exercise should ever be painful, and if you have any concerns at all about your health or physical ability, you should consult your doctor before undertaking any form of extra exercise.

The following exercises are advised particularly for endurance riders as they flex the muscles which are most likely to become shortened, primarily those in the hips. When attempting them, do not bounce, and do them only until you feel the relevant muscle gently stretching. These exercises should ideally be performed when your muscles are warm, so an ideal time is directly after riding or after you have warmed up first. Warm-ups can consist of nothing more complicated than jogging on the spot until you feel your muscles warming.

The **adductor stretch** is performed with feet apart and pointing forwards. Lunge sideways onto your bent knee, holding the stretch for up to a minute, then lunge the other way.

The **hamstring stretch** should be performed with your feet slightly pointing outwards. Hold your chest to your thigh with one arm. Your knee on that side will have bent – press to stretch it straighter and hold. Repeat the other way. This should not strain your back, unlike the hands-to-floor hamstring stretch.

Hip flexor stretch: endurance riders get very tight in the hip flexors due to the repetitive nature of the sport. However, hip flexor suppleness is essential for a legs-under riding position, which you need to be able to support yourself and not sit heavily. One foot should point forwards, the other 90° sideways. Keep the body upright and lunge gently sideways, over the outwards pointing foot, bending your knee. You will feel the stretch in the groin of the other leg. Hold and repeat the other way.

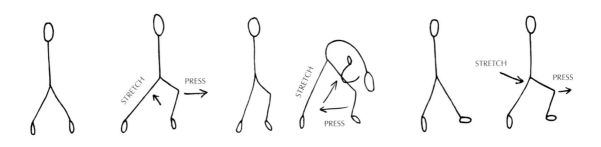

ADDUCTOR STRETCH   HAMSTRING STRETCH   HIP FLEXOR STRETCH

Suppling work

These exercises, performed regularly and correctly, should help to supple muscles which are regularly used for riding. Suppling exercises can also be performed in the saddle, ideally in an enclosed area and with someone to hold your horse for you.

Starting at the top, head and neck exercises help to supple your neck, reducing tension and increasing your awareness of how you carry your head. Drop your head to your chest and circle it gently both ways, tipping it as far back as possible to look behind you when you reach the top of the circle.

Arm and shoulder exercises help to increase your balance and confidence in the saddle. Start by shrugging and circling your shoulders – again, this is good for reducing tension.

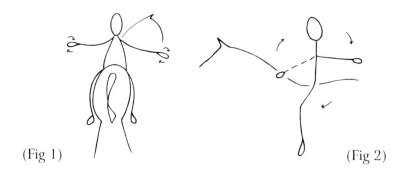

(Fig 1)   (Fig 2)

Raise your arms with your hands out to the sides and perform small circles. This helps to strengthen your shoulders and improve posture. (Fig 1)

Now stretch your arms out in front of you and circle them above your head and round to your sides, forwards and backwards, all the time reaching as far as you can. (Fig 2)

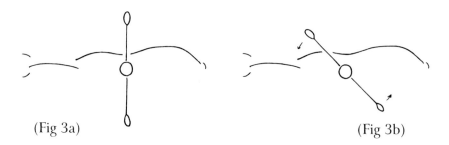

(Fig 3a)   (Fig 3b)

Stretching your arms out sideways again, twist either way, reaching as far behind you each time as you can. (Figs 3a, 3b). This supples and stretches your torso and abdominals. The same muscles can also be strengthened by (Fig 4a) leaning forwards towards your horse's ears and trying to touch your forehead on his neck, keeping your hands on your hips; (4b) trying to touch your toes (but make sure that your legs stay still!); then (4c) leaning back to touch your horse's rump with the back of your hat.

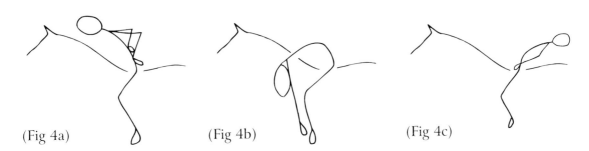

(Fig 4a)   (Fig 4b)   (Fig 4c)

To deepen your seat, take your feet out of the stirrups and pull your heels up in front of you to find your seatbones (Fig 5a), then take your feet in your hands and pull them up behind you (Fig 5b). Lifting your legs away from the saddle sideways (Fig 6) helps to strengthen inner and outer thigh muscles; and circling your feet, pointing them as far down as possible, helps to stretch calves and ankles.

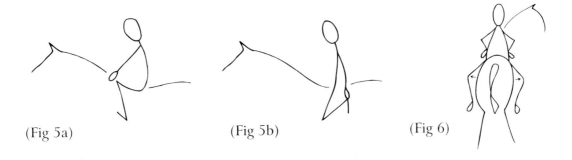

(Fig 5a)   (Fig 5b)   (Fig 6)

Cardiovascular work

Having performed the above simple routine once, you will probably be made only too aware of how stiff and inflexible you have actually become through riding itself! You are likely, also, to be surprised when you attempt some aerobic fitness work how limited your riding fitness actually is. Your own aerobic work should perform the same functions as it does in your horse – training your entire system to become more efficient and function more effectively. It is of paramount importance that you breathe properly during aerobic work – panting at the top of your lungs only has limited effect in providing enough oxygen for your system to work and will result in you not getting the best out of the exercise. Twenty minutes of aerobic work two or three times a week will have, within a few weeks, a marked effect on your general fitness and ability to cope with sustained riding – or whatever else may come your way during an endurance ride!

Working with your horse

As the terrain covered on a ride often involves dismounting and walking or running with your horse, this is perhaps the most logical exercise to start practising at home. Whenever I take a horse out training I dismount half way through the work-out, or as soon as I feel warmed through. This generally only happens after the horse has had a period of warming up in walk and then some sustained steady trot, which works my body more and warms me up, so this is usually about three-quarters through a training session.

Early in the season I get off and run steadily, occasionally slowing down to walk briskly for a breather, until I feel that I'm reaching my limit, then I get back on. This might only be around ten minutes initially if you're not used to the work. You will reach the same point as your horse does when he is attempting to replenish an oxygen debt, and will feel the need to slow up and breathe hard. Never run until you are worn out, as your riding will undoubtedly suffer. During the competitive season, when my horse and I have both reached a maintenance level of fitness, I am accustomed to running several miles alongside my horse during each session.

Running technique

It is worth making the point that you need to be as careful about your own running as you are your horse's work. Running over rough, deep or rutted ground is only for the fit – you need to spend six to eight weeks on good, even going which is not too hard, to gradually condition your own body. Running exercises your entire body, not just your legs – your upper body, shoulders and arms receive a work-out too. It must always be done in a balanced way. Concentrate on keeping your body relaxed but upright without rolling from side to side or leaning forward too much.

Swing your legs through from the hip with as straight a limb flight as you are able and try to place your feet on the ground facing forwards. Keep your paces even and rhythmic, and run as lightly and smoothly as possible, placing your weight evenly on each foot. Keep your head balanced above your spine – tipping it forwards or backwards will alter your centre of balance. To illustrate this, picture your horse working with his head down – he will be on his forehand; and, with his head back in the

A fit rider making life easier and faster for her horse over a tricky downhill section at the Golden Horseshoe ride on Exmoor.

air, he will be hollow. The same applies to you: an unbalanced head carriage will serve to create pain in your neck, back, and shoulders, as well as shortening your stride.

If you are running with your horse, hold the buckle end of your reins in the hand nearest your horse, without interfering with his mouth, and without disturbing your stride and posture. If your horse will not jog beside you and stay relaxed so that you have to keep checking him or watching him, your running will become unbalanced and uneven. Try swapping sides – you might be surprised to find that you are actually tensing the shoulder of the rein-holding arm. When you have finished, shake your arms and legs gently and stretch a little to release the muscles, rather than leaping straight back on your horse. You may find that you need to lengthen your stirrups when you get back on as your legs have stretched away from their shortened, riding position.

To run effectively you also need shock-absorbing footwear and, just as uneven wear of your horse's shoes tells tales about his physical development and carriage, so it does your own! If your heels wear down excessively to one side, your foot placement is uneven to the outside or inside. If this is not due to a physical problem of your own, it will soon cause one and if you have twinges on one side or in certain muscle groups, get yourself videoed to enable yourself to even up your action and posture.

Other aerobic work

Walking and running up hills are as effective for you as for your horse, and as running is free and can be done wherever you ride your horse, it is probably the most accessible and useful form of aerobic exercise for endurance riders. Riding either side of your run also enables your body to warm up and cool down gently. However, some people detest running and prefer to swim or cycle, walk their dogs briskly, walk on a treadmill in a gym, or take part in a formal aerobics class. Whatever form of aerobic work you undertake, aim to perform a minimum of 20 minutes, ideally building up to 30 or 40 minutes, three times a week. Always warm up and cool down gently either side of your session to minimise the risk of strains.

Fuel for fitness

Following the same principles as for your horse, it is as important to fuel your body correctly for the work that you do as it is to feed your horse properly. Your own weight should be kept to an optimum, as should your horse's. Having said this, we have a choice over what to feed ourselves, whereas our horses are fed a set menu and don't have to contend with the same temptations that we do! It can be difficult to control your own diet and weight, but it is worth remembering that you are likely to need occasional treats or deviations from what is strictly good for you. This might not just be due to your own cravings, but can be as a result of social pressures, whether it be having a beer in the pub, cooking for a family, eating ice-cream on a hot day or not looking rude at a dinner party! Enlist the support of those around you – you will be surprised how much easier controlling your intake is if people cease to put temptation in your way! However, you owe it to your horse to try and control your own diet and weight as effectively as possible, without becoming puritanical about it.

Cutting out the fat and providing more energy

Most of us are fairly well aware of the basics of a healthy, balanced diet. These include cutting back on fat and protein-rich foods and eating more starch, fibre (in the form of fruit and vegetables) and drinking plenty of fluid, ideally water. The current thinking is that excesses of sugar and salt should also be avoided, although cutting either out altogether is just as detrimental to your health as is eating too much. Remember that fat comes in unexpected forms and, although some fat is necessary in the diet, it is easy to forget all the dollops of butter, oil (even in salad dressings), slurps of full-fat milk, mayonnaise, pieces of cheese, bars of chocolate, biscuits, alcoholic drinks (which are very high in calories from sugar) or handfuls of peanuts. Processed foods like crisps, cakes and pies also contain deceptively high levels of fat. Margarine is no better for you than butter – it generally contains high levels of trans-fatty acids due to the hydrogenation process, which act similarly to saturated fats.

Today there is little difference in taste between low and full-fat foods and, as with any habit, you will find that once the initial switch has been made, you will prefer the new foods and feel better for the change. Replace all the high-fat foods with skimmed milk, low-fat spread, oil-free dressings, half-fat cheese, and lean meat. Fill the gaps with starchy, high carbohydrate foods like bread, rice, jacket potatoes (or potatoes cooked anyhow, as long as it is without fat!) and pasta, even in pre-prepared dishes. These foods are high in carbohydrate and provide energy for exercise. Bread also contains protein, and high-fibre foods like many breakfast cereals, baked beans, jacket potatoes, sweetcorn and wholemeal pasta will set you well on the way to providing your body with all it needs to perform as you wish it to.

Other requirements

As with your horse's diet, protein levels are often over-emphasised. A basis of starchy food, with fruit and vegetables next, protein for some interest and fat kept to a minimum will help you to receive a good balance of vitamins, minerals and trace elements. Fruit is an underestimated source of fuel for the body – apart from its water and fibre content, fruit contains plenty of vitamins and minerals. Supplementation is rarely necessary for the average person unless the diet is deficient, for example in iron if you don't eat red meat or another adequate source, some B vitamins in vegetarians, calcium and sometimes phosphorus in vegans. Vitamins C, E, A and selenium are also anti-oxidants and are therefore essential for dealing with free-radicals.

Most people manage perfectly well on between 2000 and 2500 calories per day between ages fifteen and seventy. As you age, your metabolism slows slightly, reducing the need for calorific intake; if you are trying to lose weight, decrease your intake to 1500 or 1000 calories minimum per day. However, increased exercise demands increased calorific intake, although it also trains your body to become more efficient at using the food provided. You will need to experiment with a working daily diet, just as you do for your horse. Remember that on his days off, he has his feed cut down – but do you? Again, quality rather than quantity is the key and you may need to increase the carbohydrate-rich food you eat.

Fuel to compete

During a ride, you will need to maintain your energy levels just as your horse does and will need regular carbohydrate intakes, in whatever form you prefer. Glycogen before, during and after a ride will spare your body's reserves, and can be taken in the form of bananas, yoghurt, bread pudding, porridge or cereals, low-fat flapjacks, pasta, dried fruit and nuts. There are several proprietary carbohydrate bars and drinks available to do this efficiently and I personally find these very useful. Often they contain slow- and fast-burn carbohydrates, so that their effects are balanced and sustained.

Fluid intake

Experiment and find out what works for you; read the labels and beware of drinks which are actually just gimmicks and full of sugar. Of course, it is essential that you also drink to maintain fluid levels within your body, but if you are eating you may find that plain water or water with a carbohydrate boost eliminates the need for extra minerals or electrolytes. If you become dehydrated, all sorts of physical symptoms ensue, which can be disastrous for your riding. Hangovers are actually largely due to dehydration – imagine competing with a hangover and you will understand why it is so important to keep taking in fluids all the while. Stick to still drinks; fizzy or carbonated drinks just fill your stomach with gas and prevent it from taking in as much fluid.

During a ride

In the build-up to a ride, continue to ride, exercise and eat as normal. However, during the day or so beforehand, many riders find it beneficial to cut down on exercise slightly whilst maintaining their carbohydrate intake, to gain some reserve on which to work during the ride. The night before a ride you should certainly try to avoid any alcohol, which will dehydrate you, and eat as balanced a meal as possible – plenty of carbohydrate and fibre, a little protein, and a minimum of fat and sugar. Start drinking plenty of fluids now, to make sure that you are as fully hydrated as you need to be. On ride mornings, eat some breakfast – baked beans on toast, bananas and creamed rice, porridge or cereal and milk – whatever you find to be the best way of getting the carbohydrate in. Drink as much as possible before you set out. During a 25-mile ride, you should attempt to keep sipping at fluid and take in 0.5-0.75litre (1-1½ pints), more so on a hot or dry day. During a 100-miler, your fluid intake will vastly increase, just as your horse's does.

If you use a carbohydrate/mineral balanced drink, eat whatever tempts you, but if you drink plain water then your diet should contain plenty of carbohydrate and minerals. Once you get off, keep drinking and eating to enable your system to recover as quickly as possible. The day after a ride, or for a few days following it, your body will tell you what it is deficient in – I know plenty of people who keep eating small pasta meals or sandwiches and bananas during their recovery time. You will be surprised at how thirsty you will feel, even if you have been drinking during the ride. Using proprietary energy bars and drinks can help to take some of the guesswork out of your diet at this time, and prevent the feeling of craving certain foods, which is due to a deficiency within the body. For example, if you crave bananas, you may be lacking potassium; if you crave liver, apricots or chocolate, you may be needing some extra iron; if you crave oranges and tomatoes, you may need more vitamin C. Even at home, your regime should continue – when you come back from riding, don't head for the biscuit tin, but make some toast or a sandwich instead and drink a glass of water.

Staying sharp

There used to be many riders who refused to eat during a ride, or who neither ate nor drank. If you take nothing in, your mental alertness and physical functioning will suffer greatly and you may become somewhat unco-ordinated. If you see frowning riders on the trail yelling at their crews or slapping their horses, you can bet they are dehydrated or haven't eaten. If you are still one of the culprits, try a carbohydrate drink, banana or some other fruit, or even a sandwich as you are riding – you will feel a marked difference in your performance and well-being. Often this will manifest itself during a ride as simply feeling happier, more confident and better able to cope, and afterwards your recovery will be faster than if your entire system was depleted.

There is no doubt that good nutrition and physical fitness helps you to stay mentally sharper, more alert and better able to make decisions than an unfit, under- or malnourished rider. At home during training, but more importantly during a ride, you need to be able to pick up the signals that your horse sends about his own well-being, stress levels and state of mind in order to manage and ride him correctly. This is simply not possible if you are either not functioning properly due to lack of food or fluid. Often riders blame their inability to take in food or fluid on nerves, which can also be debilitating through preventing you from focusing on the task in hand and the riding of the route and your horse. Some riders are too nervous to sleep properly the night before a ride, which can be really detrimental during a long day's physical work.

Keeping a focus

Top riders have learned to focus and pick up the tiniest clues from their horses. There are all sorts of strategies to enable you to turn your anxiety into a positive mental attitude, and again, it is a question of experimenting to find out what works best for you. The most vital point

Michelle Aldridge making it look easy. A fit rider is more able to help her horse to cope with the distance, even at the end of a long or hot ride.

to remember is that this is your hobby and it is supposed to be fun! The next thing to remember is that during this time, it is up to you to make the most of your preparation at home, and that you need to relax, think positively and focus in order to do that. Most of us get nervous at some point during a ride, more so when racing or when the outcome of a ride is important to you. I always find that a mass start and waiting for vettings are my worst times.

You need to learn to find strategies to enable you to cope with these nerves rather than letting them get in your way. The most positive way to do this is to give yourself something else to think about, ideally something related to the task in hand. During a mass start my worry is that my horse will go berserk and I'll lose control. Instead of becoming stiff as a board and being frightened of the horse, I tell myself that the horse is obviously far more worried than I am about the whole situation (otherwise he wouldn't be so up tight) and that as I have got us into this situation, it is up to me to relax the horse and keep him calm enough to listen to me.

Throughout my training and preparation at home, my whole approach is to have a relaxed but interested animal, and I try to maintain that approach throughout the ride. While nervous competitors are pounding big circles warming up, you might ride a few figures of eight, serpentines or circles of different sizes, to give you both something else to think about and focus your minds on your work. During the actual line-up, think forward, which relaxes your posture and seat, so relaxing the horse, rather than tensing to fight the horse. Talk to him and concentrate on keeping him calm rather than turning inwards to your own worries – this is always extremely beneficial.

Once you are moving, you will find that the majority of your concerns are over and it's a ball from then on. Concentrate on motivation to perform, rather than anxiety preventing action, and cultivate a calm outlook under duress, which should help to keep your horse relaxed. You need to focus on and look to your horse at all times to be able to provide the best management possible for him. During the wait for presentation to a vet, I keep completely away from the horse and trust him to my crew entirely, using the time to sit, breathe deeply, eat, drink and try to shut off and relax, thinking about the next section of the route. You may be surprised to see riders apparently unconcerned about what is going on – but look at their horses and you will see that they are just as blasé. The difference is that the rider is probably quaking inside, whilst the horse thinks it's all in a day's work. Those closest to you will know how wound up you are, but it is essential that the horse does not.

In order to keep the horse this relaxed, it is important to know your job and to have prepared adequately beforehand. Everything that you can do to enable the ride to pass as easily as possible is advantageous – including having organised yourself and your crew as well as possible prior to the ride.

8

The Back-up Crew

Although endurance riding in the UK is not impossible without a crew, many ride rules do not permit riders to take part without a helper of some kind. On any ride, a fast, efficient crew can make the difference between Best Condition or just finishing, and winning or losing. Your horse's management will be of a much higher standard than if you were going solo. On long, hot or difficult rides, your crew can be the only thing that keeps you going. Most high-mileage riders will tell you that it would all be impossible without their crew and that all they (the rider) have to do is ride. It is important, therefore, to consider yourself – the rider – as part of the team which gets your horse round; you have the role of jockey or pilot. It is also vital to prepare and organise the whole team so that your horse receives the best possible management on the day.

Essential qualities

Potential crew members can be found wherever there are horses, and even in plenty of places where there aren't! It is extremely important to have the right kind of person taking charge of you and your horse. Most riders start out with their nearest and dearest as their only crew member. This may be a spouse or partner, parent, eldest child, or best friend. The most vital factor about your crew is that they care about the horse and form some sort of understanding with him. If your crew is not interested in taking care of their charge, there is little point in bullying them into going along and, over short distances, you will probably work better alone.

In order to do the best for your horse, you need to try and find a team who will support your efforts and enjoy the whole event. Apart from commitment, interest and reliability, it is important that your crew is calm, has some common sense and a practical approach. If you are just starting out, it is not vital that you have someone who is experienced with horses; as long as they are competent, you will learn together how best to care for your horse.

At higher mileages and faster speeds, however, you need someone who can read you and your horse as well as, if not better than, you can, and who is able to take complete charge of you both. Once you have been competing for some time and ride higher mileages or want to race, you will need to delegate certain responsibilities and relinquish much of the physical management of the ride to your crew, so it is essential that you trust them implicitly. People need to be physically fit and agile to cope with your horse, carrying buckets and equipment, and with attending to you both during a long day. You also need at least one good driver to get everybody from A to B, and ideally to drive you to the venue, and home again when you are worn out afterwards. It's a tall order!

Teamwork

You all need to be able to work together, take and give orders from and to each other, and think logically and calmly about the immediate situation. There is no place for temper, messing about, or for someone who doesn't pull his weight. Some of the best crews are not initially horsey, but soon become so, and they certainly don't have to be riders. The first thing your crew needs to do is to learn a little about your horse, strike up a rapport and for you all to get on with each other. It's no use having somebody brilliant if either you or your horse can't stand the sight of them! Also, as everything is done within a time limit, fast, efficient crewing is essential. Racing can put pressure on everyone and at a vet

Teamwork that runs as smoothly as clockwork: Jackie Taylor's crew, Pete and Sam, working on the phenomenally successful Sally. There's no need for words: this routine is second nature to an efficient crew.

gate, your crew will be competing against others to present your horse first. In these situations, you need people who will concentrate, listen, stay calm and work together.

The team bond which comes between horse, rider and crew evolves slowly over several seasons' competition. I only use a different crew if it is completely essential that I take part in a ride, and there is absolutely no possibility that even one of my own crew can come; this has only happened to me a few times. Most riders rely completely on their crew to be there when both horse and rider need them most for physical and moral support. Team spirit becomes very strong and your crew play a major part in motivating you and your horse, letting you know where you are for time or in the field and in many cases dictating exactly how to ride.

The observer's eye

There is enormous value in having an observer's eye upon you and your horse; someone who sees you every few miles is in an ideal position to judge how you are both coping. Your crew also needs the ability to be able to act upon those observations, and you need to take heed. For example, if they say you look tired and tell you to eat, then eat! If they tell you to slow down, slow down. If they think your horse is lame or tired, pull up. It's easy to see why so many riders feel that a good crew is as rare as a good endurance horse and I, for one, have to agree.

Preparation at home

All of this makes it sound as though you need vast numbers of super-human endurance experts if you are going to be able to manage at all! Few of us have access to a trained crew or even to experienced riders, however, and need to enlist the help of those around us. You can maximise anyone's ability through a little practice and by doing plenty of groundwork before the ride. Initially all your crew needs to do is get to know your horse and become accustomed to handling him. One of my crew actually started out being quite afraid of horses but now happily picks out feet, walks the horse and cools him down without batting an eye.

It is a good idea to either start your only, inexperienced crew at short rides or, if you're bringing in a new member, make sure that you have another more experienced crew member who can show him the ropes. This way the newcomer will learn how your horse copes with the distances, terrain, hazards and weather; how he likes to be handled, how he looks when fresh, tired or unsound; how he reacts to certain handling and management, and how to keep him calm and relaxed. The first thing that creates an instant bond between any stranger and your horse is finding that itchy spot that every horse has – show a stranger where it is and you'll see what I mean.

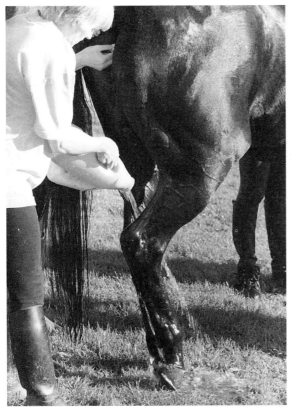 

Pouring water over the large blood vessel in a hind leg, helping to cool down the horse. The other crew member is taking the horse's temperature. Make sure that your crew are confident about working around your horse and won't be too frightened, for example of being kicked, to work effectively.

Everything stops while the horse takes the opportunity to drink. The rider has just finished sloshing from on top while the crew has a drink ready for the rider.

Assigning roles

If you have only one crew member, he needs to be multi-talented, and you need to accept that he cannot do everything at the same time, or as fast as a team of three would. It helps to have two people if at all possible, to prevent your lone crew from getting bored, tired or lost – driving with a map in one hand is far from easy! It's also helpful to have someone to help get equipment etc. out of your vehicle and load up again whilst one does the work; or one person to hold the horse and the other to attend to it, or one person to crew the horse and one person to take care of you. Hundred-mile race riders often use two or three vehicles leapfrogging each other. One society has now changed its rules to limit riders below 50 miles to one car each, preventing wear and tear to the countryside and traffic congestion around ride routes and venues.

Ideally for rides of 40 miles and over I like to have three people; one rider crew and timekeeper, and two horse crew, one of whom is driver, the other navigator. Apart from these basic roles you need a team manager who will keep everyone together, decide your riding strategy, make decisions and help to motivate everyone. You also need to decide who will perform which tasks before you even think about going to a ride. It can be fairly easy to assign roles; in the simplest terms, whoever owns the vehicle that you are using for crewing is most likely to be the driver. The person who is least experienced or least horse-confident should be your rider crew, and the person who is most experienced will be your main horse crew. Someone happy to handle the horse but still learning might be the only one who holds the horse, offers it buckets of feed and drink, but leaves the hands-on servicing to the more horse-minded crew member. Someone who is quick with his hands will be better at dealing with your horse than someone who takes a while to think about fetching things or remember where to find them. The strongest person will naturally be best at carrying heavy buckets of water; the calmest, quietest person will be best for presenting your horse to the vet.

Ride preparation

Once you have a driver, you need a navigator for the route. At home in preparation for the ride, your navigator will soon come out of the closet – they'll be the one who looks up how to get to the venue first and finds the best route there! As soon as you have your paperwork for any ride, get your crew together and sit down with the map. As the rider, it is up to you to have a large-scale Ordnance Survey map with the route traced on to it, ideally in fluorescent pen, with the checkpoints, vet stops, and start and finish marked on it. Your pre-ride work should include learning to read a map. Spend some time studying the map keys to familiarise yourself with the symbols. Then, study the ride terrain and think about how to ride it in as much detail as possible before the event.

Speeds and timing

Next, work out the distances for each leg of the ride, be it between checkpoints, vet stops, or radio stewards. Use a map wheel or, failing that, a piece of cotton to measure the distances. Work out how long it will take you to ride each leg at various speeds: for example, if you wish to ride at 8mph, divide 60 minutes by 8 miles, which is 7.5 minutes for each mile. At 12mph, 60 divided by 12 gives you 5 minutes for each mile. Multiply your minute formula by the number of miles in each leg; for example, if the distance from the start to your first checkpoint is 3.4 miles, at 8mph this will take you 3.4 x 7.5 mins per mile = 25.5 minutes.

Checkpoint		Miles	Time				
			6mph	6½mph	7mph	7½mph	8mph
CP 1	South Water	2¾	0.27	0.25	0.24	0.22	0.21
CP 2	Partridge Green	8	1.20	1.13	1.08	1.04	1.00
CP 3	Henfield	10¼	1.42	1.34	1.27	1.22	1.16
CP 4	Partridge Green	12½	2.05	1.55	1.47	1.40	1.37
CP 5	South Water	17¾	2.57	2.43	2.32	2.22	2.13
	Westons Farm	20½	3.25	3.09	2.56	2.44	2.34
Finish	Total time elapsed		3.25	3.09	2.56	2.44	2.34

A timetable for a 20-mile ride at a set speed of between 6 and 8mph. Checkpoints are named and marked with mileages and elapsed time in minutes and hours. The tighter the speed restriction, the more careful you need to be about timing. Race rides are much easier in this respect!

If the ride restricts crewing access, work out your speeds from each access point to the next. I usually work out three sets of speeds for a timed ride, i.e. the slowest, fastest, and an average, so that my crew can tell me what speed I'm doing. In practice, with experience, you will know what speed you are riding at, but to start with you may prefer to carry the tables with you. I always give my crew a copy, as riding time across country means nothing to someone driving a completely different route and, should you be late through getting lost or injured, they will know when to raise the alarm.

Meeting points

Study the terrain for each leg to decide if your times are realistic; if there is a lot of road work or steep hills, you will need to increase each leg time accordingly. Next, sit down with your crew and look at the map. Obviously, your primary navigator will need to be able to read the map, too, and so should your driver, who will best be able to decide if he can make your times or not. Are the checkpoints accessible for crewing? Are they too close or too far apart? Where else could you meet? I usually like to be met a minimum of every 4 or 5 miles, unless I am riding too fast and it is impossible for the crew to reach me in time.

Your navigator needs to find the shortest route possible between each meeting place and either remember this from your consultation or write down directions for the day. Always remind them to make use of landmarks in an emergency – for example, if your meeting place is near a

This was a ride route map and timetable used by my own crew on a 60-mile race ride, which I was aiming to complete at around 8mph. The actual times, in brackets, were written by the crew on the day. The circled times are vet-gate hold times. As you can see, I rode the first 15 miles steadily to warm up, then picked up to half way, rode steadily out of the half-way vet and picked up again around 45 miles to finish at roughly the right speed. This ride was the horse's first 60, and we came a delighted third!

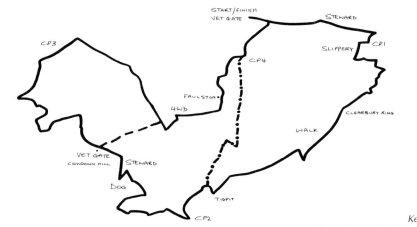

Key
Main outline – 40-mile race
Long dashes – Diversion for 30-mile route
Dots and dashes – Diversion for 20-mile route

8 mph	1st lap			2nd lap	(4.32)
START	12.00		LEAVE	4.35	
STEWARD 2.25 miles	12.17		32.25 miles	4.51	(5.07)
CP1		(12.28)	CP1		
CLEARBURY RING 7.5 miles	12.56	(1.10)	37.5 miles	5.31	(5.56)
TIDPIT 13.75 miles	1.43		43.75 miles	6.18	
15.5 miles	1.56		45.5 miles	6.31	
CP2	✷ NO CREWS ALLOWED	(2.10)	CP2		(6.44)
17.5 miles	2.11		47.5 miles	6.46	
STEWARD 19.5 miles	2.26		49.5 miles	7.01	
VG1 COWDOWN HILL 21.5 miles	2.34 2.41 (+20) LEAVE 3.01	(2.58)	VG3 51.5 miles	7.16 (+20) 7.36 OUT	(+15 mins) (7.32)
23.5 miles	3.16		53.5 miles	7.51	
FAULSTON 25.75 miles	3.33		55.75 miles	8.08	(8.05)
CP4 28.25 miles	✷ NO CREW – NO TIME TO MEET 3.51		58.25 miles	8.26	
VG2 (½ way) 30 miles	(+30) 4.05		60 miles	8.40	

church marked on the map, if all else fails, head for the nearest church and see if the map matches the scenery! Some riders' biggest fear is getting lost on a ride. It is worth mentioning that you will never go very far out of your way before someone notices your absence, even if you don't notice that you have strayed yourself, which you are bound to do if there is a shortage of markers. Emergency map-reading on the hoof should also help you to learn to navigate and work out exactly where you are in relation to the landmarks around you.

Once you have arranged your meeting places, you need to stick to them as closely as possible, although in some cases this may not be possible and your crew needs to get to you somewhere else. Inexperienced crew members can easily underestimate your horse's need for fluids, feed and care during a ride as well as your own. It is therefore wise to arrange more meeting places than are necessary than to have too few and have a dehydrated, hot or tired horse. The main point of having a crew is to ensure that you both get round sound and well and, when racing, that you get round faster than anyone else. The next thing to practise at home with your crew are some basic management methods during the ride.

Team management

It helps if your crew can load and unload your horse, in case for any reason you can't do the job yourself. In practice, you should always do this task unless you are injured or elsewhere. The next thing you need to decide is who presents the horse to the vet, and who trots the horse up for the vet. If you have one calm crew member who also does a good trot-up, you're well set. Otherwise, you need to decide who does what best and take that one person with you, or leave the vetting to two selected people and stay out of the way altogether, particularly if you are on edge. I prefer to present the horse for the first vetting myself, then hang around within earshot for the rest so I can hear the vet's comments. In practice your crew may prefer you out of the way – mine always tell me I look so worried that the vets will be convinced that there must be something wrong with the horse! Some riders prefer to do the whole lot themselves.

Trotting up

I always prefer to watch the trot-up so that I can see how my own horse is going, but in order to do this you do need someone with whom the horse will trot well. My first vetting sees me holding the horse and keeping him calm, and answering any queries the vet may have while he inspects him. Then, I hand over to my best crew member for the trot-up.

Your horse needs to trot out actively but in a controlled way, with a good length of rein and without any interference from the handler.

Train your horse and crew to perform as close to the classic trot-up as is possible – and not to spook at cones.

When trotting up, you should always be on the left of the horse and turn the horse away from you, towards the vet, without obscuring his view of the horse's legs.

Teach your horse to respond to voice commands of 'Ter-rot', 'Steady', and 'Whoa'. You will be asked to trot 30 metres/yards away from the vet, turn and come back – always stay by the horse's shoulder so as not to risk being mown down or getting in the vet's way. The vet wants to see that the horse is sound, so interfering with the horse's trot in any way is forbidden, and walking half of the distance is no help to anyone. Carry a crop if you are in any doubt over your control; the rules vary between societies but it is often advisable to present in a bridle, for extra control. The best way to learn how to do a good trot-up is to watch others.

Who handles the horse at later vettings will depend on how things are going. If you are racing or are trying to return as low a pulse rate as possible, a steady but active trot is important. Post-ride vetting rules vary but at some rides your horse's pulse will only be taken once before you trot him up and not again afterwards. In this case, as fast and active a trot as possible will impress the vets and prevent the horse from being lazy. Keep an eye on the surface of the trot-up; if it is slippery or stony go as steadily as possible. Finally, if you are asked to trot more than once – don't panic. The vet may just be familiarising himself with your horse's action.

Other vetting procedures

Whilst the vet is taking your horse's pulse, don't fiddle with your horse's nose, as uneven breaths can cause his heart rate to fluctuate. Whoever relaxes the horse most effectively should handle the horse during vetting. If one person is quicker than another at taking off rugs, let them do it. If one person is ineffective at trotting the horse out, get someone else to do it, or do it yourself. It is helpful to be near the vet to hear his comments, and always heed them – if he tells you to slow down or advises you to withdraw, do it. If he is doubtful about your horse, pull it out, unless you are 200% certain of what you are doing. There is always another day. If you are spun, don't argue. The vets are doing their utmost to prevent unfit horses from starting or continuing, and their decision is final. They will often have a more experienced eye for fatigue, dehydration or lameness than you will. Always be polite and courteous to the vet, and thank him and his writer for their time and attention, and ask your crew to do the same!

Crewing on the trail

Apart from presenting to the vet, later during the ride your crew will

Sloshing whilst on board: the rider is often in the best position to cool the horse's neck and shoulders, but practise this at home so as not to frighten your horse.

An efficient crew making the most of the ford at Tarr Steps to keep the horse cool.

actually be attending to your horse on the route. You can practise what you are going to do, who does what and how before you go, so that on the day there is no confusion.

At rides of short distances, all they need to do is offer your horse a drink, sponge or slosh him down to keep him cool, and attend to anything else which may arise, such as picking out his feet if you have covered a particularly stony patch or washing him off if he is especially muddy or sweaty. As you progress to longer rides at faster speeds, your horse will need to be offered feed at every opportunity, as well as water and electrolytes, and will need to be kept sloshed off or washed down to cool him. The fastest way to get cold water onto your horse's skin is by pouring it from a slosh bottle – the type that contain fabric conditioner or liquid washing detergent are best as they usually have a big handle, are sturdy, with a wide top and a lid that your crew can easily pull off when they see you coming.

Crewing a race

If you are racing, your meetings with your crew may often see you trotting past without a break in stride as they run alongside to pass you up

Expert crew member and ride vet Tony Pavord, in action during an international race. He is running beside the rider to pass up a much-needed slosher.

a slosh bottle. It can be a good idea to station two people 30 or 40 metres/yards apart, so that you can grab two sloshers in quick succession, or a drink for yourself if you are not carrying one with you. Your horse will have to get used to you dropping or throwing empty bottles about the place!

Your crew should prepare for meeting you by having available water and electrolytes, an energy boost if you use one, feed, sloshers, a sponge for washing off sweat and mud, a hoof pick, and food and drink for you. Ask them to have ready whatever you might need for your next meeting, such as a change of gloves, Vaseline (for chafed skin) or wound powder.

As they watch you approach and ride away, they should be looking for signs that either you or your horse need attention in some way, and to keep an eye on your general condition. Whoever is keeping an overall watch on your position or speed should be able to update you when you see him.

Vet-gate technique

Apart from attending to you both out on the course, your crew will have to prepare your horse for vetting. The rules vary between societies and it is as well to be sure of the procedure before you get to the ride. Again, you can practise quick and efficient vet-gate technique at home. This is when your crew will learn most about managing your horse and you need your time-keeper to have an eye constantly on the clock to make sure that you keep tabs on elapsed riding time and hold time.

The first thing to do as you arrive at a vetting or gate is for you to dismount and for someone to hold the horse and offer him a drink, while someone else takes the pulse. On a timed ride with a break before vetting, walk him gently to prevent him stiffening up and manage him according to the weather and his temperature; if he is cold, find some shelter, rug him up and don't slosh him with water. If he's hot, get him into some shade and keep applying cold water to his neck, shoulders and front legs and keep it iced, if you have ice in a cool box.

If you have to wait for your vetting, this is the time to change the horse's saddle pad and girth, get yourself a drink and some food, and keep the horse walking gently and relaxed. Only feed him after a vetting because eating will raise his pulse rate. Be ready to mount and continue at the end of the allotted waiting time, or leave straight away, as soon as possible after vetting if it is included in your riding time.

If you have time before presenting or if the horse's pulse is too high, use those minutes to attend to washing off mud and sweat, although your horse must be kept warm as the cooling procedure takes place (this sounds contradictory, but the heat has to disperse from muscles slowly otherwise the horse will get stiff). At a vet gate, your riding time will not stop until you have presented to the vet and passed successfully, so your time-keeper needs to keep a check on all this in order to have you ready following your hold to continue with the ride. If, however, you are able to present straight away, this provides plenty of time for your horse to relax, eat and drink and have his girth and saddle pad changed. Your crew will learn either to keep him in the shade or shelter, keep him still or moving, fuss him or ignore him the more rides you attend and the better accustomed you all become to each other. Your time-keeping crew will let you know when to be ready, and you and your team manager should confer to decide how to tackle the next section while the other crew pack away the equipment into the crewing vehicle.

The crew vehicle

The type of crew vehicle you have will largely depend upon what is available to you and what transport you use for your horse. Crewing from a horsebox is banned by some societies and is actually very difficult and slow anyway. Check how many crew vehicles you are allowed under the race rules before you go. Most of us aspire to some kind of four-wheel drive vehicle and a trailer, as you can unhitch and leave the trailer at the ride venue, leaving behind anything you don't need. An estate car, Land Rover, small van or rough terrain vehicle is ideal. A smart vehicle could soon be spoiled, as it will get muddy, gritty, may be thrashed along tiny country lanes, and will take a battering from your equipment and possibly even from your horse! You are likely to use lots of fuel, so diesel engines are favoured for their economy. Other desirable features include plenty of space inside for passengers and easy access to a boot for equipment; the vehicle must also be reliable and easy to run and maintain.

Equipment Checklist – Crew

✓ water carriers (large buckets with lids will do)
✓ buckets for drinking and washing down
✓ slosh bottles
✓ sponges and sweat scrapers
✓ feed, electrolytes, energy boost
✓ rider's drinks and food
✓ times, map, stop-watch, notebook and pen (for route
     instructions, keeping tabs on vet parameters)
✓ hoof pick
✓ spare set of shoes for your horse
✓ waterproof clothing for the rider
✓ Easyboot
✓ spare numnah and girth or girth sleeve
✓ any other spares you need, e.g. whip, gloves, half-chaps etc.
✓ ice if it's hot
✓ insect repellent
✓ first-aid equipment: bandages, antiseptic, wound powder,
     Animalintex, ice-packs, Vaseline, flowers of sulphur

Whatever equipment you take along to the ride depends upon your own and your individual horse's needs, as well as the weather and distance you are riding. Everything should be designed to be easy to use and effective, as you want to take with you as little as possible. Apart from your horse's rugs and some form of spare tack, your crew will need:

In practice my crew carry a multi-purpose first-aid kit, including human

A fully-loaded crew vehicle with buckets, feed bowl and sloshers ready for a fast-moving rider. Crews tend to co-operate on parking and meeting places for riders.

and equine essentials. It is as well for everyone to know a few basic first-aid procedures which can be applied before the emergency services arrive. Riders who fall should only be moved to put them into the recovery position if necessary, then kept still. Learn how to clear someone's airway, perform mouth-to-mouth resuscitation and take a pulse. You should also know how to stem the bleeding of large wounds (in horses or humans), by applying direct pressure and trying to raise the injury site to stem the flow of blood. Always add bandages or pads on top of each other; never remove the original, as it may set the bleeding off again. Small wounds can be washed clean and dressed, but if you want the vet's attention, don't powder or spray them unless he has seen them. If you suspect a broken bone keep the casualty still. Burns should be treated with cold water only, for as long as possible, and then isolated from infection by covering with a clean plastic bag.

The essence of all first aid is to apply basic emergency care to render the patient safe, and wait for the experts to take charge. As long as you are able to stop bleeding and deal with the most basic needs of an emergency, you are well on the way to coping with most eventualities. Whatever happens on a ride, it is rarely the end of the world. If you do get lost or you or your horse are injured, the best advice is to stay put and wait for someone to find you. Another rider will come along behind you or, if not, your crew will report you late if a checkpoint steward doesn't. People will know where to look for you if you have stayed close to the route between checkpoints; attempting to find your own way back and perhaps wandering off course will only lengthen the time it takes for someone to find you. In practice, disasters rarely happen on an endurance ride.

Most minor injuries sustained by horses on rides, such as knocks, strains and bangs, are best treated with ice or left alone. Muscle fatigue can be treated with simple massage. Many riders and crews have favourite creams, gadgets and concoctions for little nicks and cuts or post-ride care. Once the horse has finished and been vetted he should be made as comfortable as possible, cleaned up and cooled down. Applying a cooling dressing, such as ice-packs or a cold gel or paste, to the legs helps to take out heat and keep swelling down. The main course of action following any ride is to relax your horse, stop pestering him, allow him to eat and drink small meals, stroll about and graze, and take him home or back to his box to rest. This is when your crew will take over completely and your rider crew should concentrate on watering and feeding you! Hopefully, your organisation and pre-ride preparation should enable you and your crew to carry off the whole event confidently and successfully. Practice and consideration will help you to prevent or deal with the majority of eventualities and enable you to have an enjoyable and successful day.

9

Starting to Compete

Now that we have looked at training, feeding, producing and managing your horse for endurance, how do you go about putting it all together and going to your first endurance ride? In reality, many of you will have come into endurance through another sport or have done some sponsored or pleasure rides and be keen to go further. Therefore, competing in itself will not be a complete novelty to either you or your horse. However, to anyone starting out in a new discipline, there are plenty of questions that you want to ask, or concerns and confusions that you would prefer to have answered, rather than turning up without a clue about what's going on!

Where to begin?

In the UK, the bulk of endurance rides take place between March and October. How and where you start will depend largely on the part of the country you live in and when rides are run by the relevant society. For example, in Scotland, rides are mostly run by the Scottish Endurance Riding Club, although at the time of writing there are a few BHS rides too. Scottish fixtures start with training and pleasure rides as early as February, and provide a good opportunity for some early season fitness work or a chance to go along and get the feel of how it works in practice. However, in the south of England, though rides are run by both the BHS and EHPS, the first rides of the season usually take place during March and are vastly over-subscribed. If, though, you are starting out in the middle of the season, say during June or July, then no matter where you are, there will be some kind of ride during those months. In any case, contact the relevant society (British Horse Society, Endurance Horse and Pony Society, Scottish Endurance Riding Club or Irish Long Distance Riding Association) and obtain all the information you can about fixtures in your area. You do not have to be a member of any society to take part in a pleasure class at an official ride, and in most cases you can also compete in 20- or 25-milers without joining.

A well-presented, happy horse and rider, with no special equipment or tack. Remember that basic requirements are minimal and you don't need anything fancy to get started.

As few people go out to buy a purpose-bred endurance horse or to buy a horse specifically for endurance unless they have been involved before, most people start out with the horse they are currently riding or own. As long as it is sound this is probably the best way to find out if you like the sport or not. As virtually any horse should be able to complete 20 or 25 miles at a slow speed, this is the best way to learn the ropes for yourself. If your horse is being ridden regularly, say four or five days a week, for ninety minutes or two hours at a time, he should be easily fit enough

A tiny pony and rider covering the ground happily and enjoying the beautiful countryside.

to attempt his first ride. If he is in completely soft condition, you will need around eight weeks to get him fit enough to complete the distance, as outlined in Chapter 4.

How to enter

Check the fixtures schedule for the relevant ride at least a month before it is due to take place. Your first ride ideally should be within an hour or so's travelling distance so that you can go there and come back on the same day, instead of having to worry about the extra trouble and expense of stabling on the first outing. For some rides you still have to send away for a schedule or, if you are not a society member, an entry form. Make sure to enclose an SAE of the right size, for your details to be returned. Whatever the closing date of the ride, which is usually around ten days before the ride takes place, send in your entry in good time. Some popular rides are over-subscribed, so the earlier you get your entry in, the more chance you have of it being accepted. Make sure you enclose a cheque and any other paperwork that is requested. You will also need a log book for your horse. These are designed primarily to prevent young and novice horses from being misused during their early seasons, and to keep a record of a horse's performance. You can get one from your relevant society.

Four weeks to go

With around four weeks to go, this is the time to start basic preparations – such as organising repairs to your transport and tack, or buying anything you are missing or that needs replacing. Basic requirements for your horse are a saddle and bridle that fits, and for you a BSI standard hat, boots with a half-inch heel (or caged-toe stirrups for other footwear), jodhpurs or riding tights and a cross-country or rugby-type shirt. You will need to organise a crew or try to arrange to take somebody with you. Now is also the time to book your farrier to come out a few days before the ride, to fit a new set of shoes. It is sensible to go to a ride with a set that has just been bedded in but without much wear, as you never know exactly how much wear and tear your shoes will take on a ride. If the schedule gives the OS map reference, buy or order a copy of the map that you need – it's no use leaving it until the last minute and then being unable to find the right map! You might also like to buy a map holder (from a camping shop) to carry your details with you as you ride.

Still with several weeks to go, it's a good idea to start riding measured stretches at home and working out your speed. This will help you to become accustomed to riding at a certain pace and, when you have to ride to speeds, you will feel far more confident knowing how to pace your horse.

A group of pleasure riders out for a day's fun with a very mixed bunch of horses, proving that anyone can have a go and enjoy it.

Two weeks to go

A couple of weeks before the ride, go out for a couple of hours or 15 miles and ride at a steady 7.5mph; this serves as your practice. You should feel confident that both of you will complete a few more miles at the same speed, without any undue stress. If you or your horse are obviously tired over this distance and speed now, put the ride off for another few weeks and do some more training at home to improve both of your fitness levels. The more preparation you do at home, the less stress there will be for all concerned on the day. This is also the time to start practising trotting your horse up for the vet, and teaching your crew to do the same; it's beneficial for all of you, including your horse. Ask someone else to perform a mock vetting, and if your horse is not used to being washed or sloshed, or drinking from a hand-held bucket, practising now will make everyone's life easier at the ride.

One week to go

With around a week to go, you will receive your entry paperwork. What this will consist of depends upon the society, but it usually includes a list of details about the ride such as classes on the day, rules, regulations and directions. There will be a photocopy of the map of the route and in some cases a talk-round, or written instructions on riding the route. There may be details of the time allowed to complete the route for your class or notification of any allowances, such as extra time for opening and closing gates. There will be details of the ride venue and any telephone numbers for use in an emergency, such as the vet or farrier. You may have a vet sheet included, which you should fill in and take with you. Your details will also include notification of your number and your vetting time, and in some cases your start time too.

Firstly, you need to sit down and work out how to get to the venue. Look at your details and, if you have any queries, ring the secretary or organiser now to clear them up. Next, study the route, work out your times and speeds, and get together with your crew to discuss where they can meet you. With a week to go, you should still be working and feeding your horse much as usual. It is too late now to do any extra fitness work, and during the last couple of days it is advisable to continue with light exercise and feed. During this week your farrier should come to fit a new set of shoes. If the old set is not very worn, keep them for spares. If not, ask for a new set to be shaped and fitted but not put on, so that you can take them with you for emergencies.

If it's cold and your horse is likely to sweat up, or if he is particularly hairy, now is a good time to clip to gain the maximum benefit for keeping his skin cool. This is also the time to make a list of anything you still need to do – such as buying supplies for the day. You should make a checklist

Ride Checklist

Horse
✓ haynet
✓ rugs
✓ saddle, girth and pad
✓ bridle
✓ headcollar and rope
✓ grooming kit (including hoof picks)

Crew
✓ water carriers
✓ drinking bucket
✓ washing bucket, sloshers, sponge and sweat scraper
✓ feed and feed bucket
✓ hoof pick
✓ first aid kit
✓ spare set of shoes
✓ any other spares you feel that you may need, e.g. reins, gloves etc.
(For a more detailed list of items for longer rides, see page 123)

Rider
✓ cash
✓ paperwork and log book
✓ hat
✓ boots
✓ gloves
✓ whip
✓ food and drink
✓ wet weather gear
✓ bum bag, if you ride with one

of everything you need to take with you, and, if you feel you are liable to forget, everything you need to do on the morning before you leave!

The day before the ride, fill up with fuel so that you don't waste time stopping in the morning, and pack your transport with all the items you need to take that you aren't going to use in the morning. Load the boot of your crewing vehicle so that the water is as close to the outside as possible, for easy access and to prevent strains for whoever tries to lift it. Keep essentials like buckets, hoof picks and first aid kit close to this, then behind load items less likely to be needed. Your tack, hat and so on can sit on top, as they will be out of the crew's way while you are riding. Often it's easier to load items you won't be using for crewing into your horse transport. In this case, the easier equipment is to get at, the less time you will waste fiddling about trying to find or direct other people to things.

There are no secrets to vetting: a regular examination of your horse's mouth is part of the general check and ensures that horses who pull don't suffer from sores or bruising.

The trot-up: it's not difficult and anyone can do it, but you have to get it right so that the vets can get a proper look at your horse.

I like to give the horse and my tack a good clean the day before a ride and, if it's going to be hot, I'll plait the horse's mane into long plaits to help keep his neck cool. All of this work saves time the following morning. Get your horse's travelling gear out and ready and, if you are likely to need it, a lunge line or whip for loading assistance. Take your horse out for a steady hour's work and give him a feed, no more or less than you would usually give for such work. Over this distance, this is all both of you should need to do to prepare for the following day. Set your alarm clock, allowing plenty of time for preparation, loading and the journey, ideally arriving around thirty minutes before your vet time. Arriving much later will mean that you have to rush around at the venue, so it's advisable to build in a little extra time.

Ride morning

On the morning of the ride, have your breakfast and feed your horse. While he's eating, hitch up the trailer if you use one or lower your lorry ramp and make sure you have everything you need. Give him a quick grooming, get him dressed to travel, load up, and you're off! When you arrive, park where you are directed to park or find a sensible space.

Ideally you should find some shelter from wind and sun, but in practice rides often start in fields or car parks so this is rarely possible. If you have a crew, ask someone to stay with your transport and leave the horse loaded up while you get your bearings. It is not ideal to unload and leave a horse tied to a piece of string, in his travelling gear, with no attendant, while lorries and trailers are driving around and horses are being loaded and unloaded everywhere. Your horse is unlikely to stay calm and will undoubtedly become distracted or upset by all the goings on. It is therefore safer to have him in the transport than at risk of getting loose.

Take your money, membership card if you are a member, log book and ride details and find the ride secretary. You are likely to have to pay a deposit for your number bib, and this is also the time to ask any last minute queries. It's a good idea to put your number on straight away. This saves you flapping it under the horse's nose as you put it on later, and prevents the risk of your putting it down and losing it. Find out how the ride is marked; some use fluorescent tape or paint spray, some use lime, some use small coloured boards. Locate the vetting and trot-up area, the farrier and tack inspector, if there is one, and the loos; and buy your long-suffering crew a cup of tea! Find the start and watch a few of the competitors in earlier classes leave, so that you can see where the timekeeper is and which way they go.

If you arrive at a big ride to do a low-mileage class and everything is already in full swing, the atmosphere and activity can be electric, with supremely fit, beautiful horses and experienced riders and crews all looking as if they could do this with their eyes shut. It is enough to make anyone starting out feel novicey and unprepared, but remember – these people began in the same way as you are doing, and we all have to start

If in doubt, ask! Well-known ride vet, Tony Pavord, is one of the many friendly faces on the endurance scene. Most people are always ready to offer help and advice so long as they are not in the middle of doing something else.

somewhere. There are no secrets, you just learn by experience.

Unload your horse, take off his travelling gear (though he might need to keep a rug on) and let him have a good look at everything. If he's a complete novice or a youngster, put a bridle on and take him for a gentle walk around, to familiarise him with all the sights, sounds and smells of a ride. The rules vary between societies, but many riders prefer to present to the vet in a bridle anyway for extra control. Concentrate on keeping the horse calm, quiet and relaxed and, as this demands that you appear calm and relaxed to him, you will find that the effect for both of you will be beneficial. Your horse will appreciate you making every effort to relax him so talk to him, sing or whistle gently, and give him lots of physical contact to make him feel secure.

If you would like other riders to be gentle with you or you are particularly worried about your horse's behaviour, a green ribbon on his tail will warn others that he is a novice, and a red ribbon warns that he might kick. Don't be afraid to make it known that you are a novice – people will be more sympathetic than if you pretend you know it all and then come unstuck. Don't be too put off by all the sleek physiques and the weird and wonderful equipment as you lead your little novice round, just do your own thing and follow your own preparation and system. Most endurance riders are an extremely friendly and helpful bunch and will be more than willing to give you advice or answer your questions, but this is best left until after they have finished AND BEEN VETTED. A nervous rider, trying to relax a horse and keep his pulse down whilst preventing him from getting stiff, will not be in a particularly approachable frame of mind!

If you are required to visit the farrier before vetting, do it now. You may have to queue – just patiently wait your turn and don't push in or get stroppy, no matter how other people behave! A few minutes before your vetting time, wander gently over to the vet, ideally with your helper in tow. If you already have your vet sheet, hand it to the vet writer when they call your number; some societies use vet cards which they will already have. The vet or the writer will ask you if they have any queries. The vet will first of all examine your horse, usually starting with his eyes and teeth, then running a hand over his back and legs, picking his feet up. Anything he feels worth noting will be marked on your vet sheet so that it doesn't appear to have happened during the ride. He may ask you about any lumps, bumps or marks your horse has at the time.

Next he will take your horse's heart rate using a stethoscope; it will usually be noted on your vet sheet, although most timed rides now have a heart rate baseline set for the day. Your reading at the start is therefore purely for interest, and to ensure that the horse does not have a problem or is over the limit for starting (64bpm). If it's cold or wet, the vet is likely to let you keep the rug on your horse during the inspection, but will ask for it to be peeled back for him to take the heart rate. Try to be efficient and not waste his time.

Finally, he will ask you to trot up; if it's a very big ride this may be done by a different vet. You must take your rug off for the trot-up. As long as everything is OK, the vet will tell you that you are fine to start.

The only problems you may encounter at this stage will be either an existing injury that the vet is unhappy about your horse working with, a heart rate over the limit, or a lame horse. Don't argue with the vet's decision; he is merely trying to prevent an unfit horse from being put under any stress. Usually, with a high heart rate, he will tell you to go away and come back ten minutes later, as it may just be due to the horse's excitement. When he has finished, thank the vet.

If everything is fine and you are starting, return to your transport. At this stage your crew can unhitch the trailer – take a piece of wood for underneath the jockey wheel in case you are on a soft field! Get your map holder, hat, whip and gloves together, and your bum bag if you use one, and tack up. Always make sure that you have change in your pocket for the phone, a phone number for somebody at the venue if possible (or a mobile if you have one), and a hoof pick at least. This is the time that your crew can use to organise their water and other equipment, and get their times and directions to hand.

On the trail

Once your horse is tacked up, get on and tighten your girth. Walk him round gently to warm him up, and cast an eye over your map or talk-round if you have one. Be ready to wait by the timekeeper a minute or so before your start time. It is a good idea if you and your crew both set your watches to a couple of minutes to twelve. As you start, thank the timekeeper, and you and your crew's watches should then read twelve o'clock. This effectively acts as a zero hour from which to calculate your riding time and speeds.

Start riding gently and quietly at a steady trot, to thoroughly warm both your horse's muscles and your own. You will see plenty of inexperienced novices belting off, flat out, along the first stretch. Don't be tempted to join them. All that will happen is that your horse will become worn out more quickly than he needs to, through wasting all his energy too early on. It is worth starting as you mean to go on, and if you pace your horse from the word go, it will conserve both of your energy and save lots of problems later on. And above all, smile. You've made it, and, at long last, you're doing the ride!

Unfortunately, you may find that your horse will not listen to you and intends to go flat out, along with the other speed merchants. You have to strike a balance between trying to get your message across to him and keeping to a safe speed, and wasting both of your energy by fighting each other. He will settle eventually, but ideally should be listening to you

A group of riders enjoying a competitive ride. Your horse needs to be able to work alone and in company without getting upset.

from the start. A horse pulling you and going too fast will risk bruising his mouth as well as suffering from fatigue, so at this stage, and particularly with a youngster, try not to get caught up with others.

Ride your own ride. Even if you ride with one or more other riders, let them go if they are faster and do not push to try and keep up, or leave them behind if they are slower. Your horse will find his own rhythm at the speed you are asking him to work at and, within reason, you should let him get on with it. Groups of horses will naturally jockey for position so, unless you want your horse to join the race, stick to your own speed and pace. If you ride safely, you are far more likely to get round sound than if you go crashing along on a horse unaccustomed to the job. Those out of control or going too fast may also miss turnings or markers, and this is often how people become lost!

Out on the trail, if there are higher-mileage classes, horses may be coming back towards you, or passing you on their second lap. Other riders moving faster may want to pass you in any case, or you may wish to pass others. The standard procedure if you want to pass someone is to wait until the track is wide enough and then call out to them to ask if it's OK to pass. Trot gently by and keep trotting gently until you are well past – don't go belting off and risk upsetting the other horse. Riders who pass you should do the same. You should always make every effort to give them room to go by as soon as you possibly can – it is highly frustrating for both horse and rider trying to keep off the heels of a slower-moving animal who won't let you by.

A novice horse being carefully and considerately brought out, the pair obviously enjoying each other's company.

If there are gates to pass through and you are with others, take it in turns to open and close them, and wait until the person closing the gate is ready before moving off. If your horse is not adept at manoeuvring around gates or the gate is heavy or in poor repair, get off. Don't waste other people's time and your own by pushing your horse backwards and forwards. If there are troughs to drink from, give your horse every opportunity to do so, and don't go flying past horses who are drinking, as it will upset them. At busy road crossings, there may be a steward to help you, whom you should obey and thank. At checkpoints, you may have to have a card marked or your number taken – ensuring that this is done is your responsibility. If you are in a group, wait your turn, make sure that your number is taken, and thank the steward.

Pit stops

When you meet your crew, they should offer your horse a drink and, if he is hot, give him a slosh off to keep him cool or wash him down. You should stand well out of the way of other riders wishing to pass, and if you ride past a horse being crewed, go by quietly so as not to upset the horse. It is worth mentioning at this point that he may not drink at all over this distance, but don't panic. If you are riding with someone who has no crew of their own, then your crew should offer their horse water and a wash down, too. Have a drink yourself and eat if you are hungry, and draw your crew's attention to anything that you feel may need looking after, for instance picking out your horse's feet after a stony section. Throughout the ride, concentrate on keeping your horse as relaxed and calm as possible, and working at a steady, rhythmic pace. Negotiate any hazards carefully and sensibly, follow the markers and you should be fine. Remember to keep changing diagonals in trot or leading legs in canter, to work your horse evenly.

A 20- or 25-mile ride will be ridden without a stop and you will be vetted following the finish. If you have ridden steadily and consistently, your pace and timing should be fine and will allow you to walk the last half mile steadily into the venue. You will be given a time by the time-keeper to present to the vet, usually around thirty minutes after finishing. After a fairly easy ride of this distance, there may be no real need for elaborate cooling and vet preparation. Take your horse's pulse and, if it is under the limit, stop worrying now. It is highly unlikely to be over the limit for this distance, unless it is extremely hot, the terrain is vertical, the horse is unsound or you have ridden in very fast. Simply untack, keep the horse warm, keep offering him water and make him comfortable by brushing or sponging off any mud and sweat. Wait for your vetting time and amble over to be ready when you are called.

After the ride

The vet will probably ask you how your ride went, and carry out the same procedure as for your first vetting. Make your horse trot out actively for him, even if he is lazy or tired. When the vet tells you you've passed, thank him and give him one of your sunniest smiles! If you are spun, the vet will probably tell you what he thinks the problem is, but he may be busy and ask you to wait until everyone has finished. Take your horse back to your transport to clear the area, and let him graze, drink and relax while you re-load your gear, before you get him kitted up to go home.

Massage his back end or walk him gently. Rub his forehead or ears to encourage him to drop his head and relax, and encourage him to stale, which will also release some tension. Give the secretary half an hour to deal with your paperwork before you return your number and collect your rosette and, in some cases, your vet sheet. Remember to get your log book signed. If you have enjoyed the ride, say so, as all the people who have made your day possible are volunteers – it will make it all

We did it! This is what it's all about – the pleasure of completing and having acheived the goal.

worth their while if you show your appreciation for their efforts.

Go home and, ideally, turn your horse out for a little while to relax before stabling him at night, if he is going to come in. He should have a fairly light supper, plenty of fresh, clear water and hay, and ideally his legs rubbed over with witch hazel or a cooling product to help take the heat out. Stop fussing now, and leave him alone to relax. Always check him last thing, just to make sure that he is relaxed and happy. The next morning, if he has stood in, he may be a little stiff, but realistically he is unlikely to suffer any ill-effects from a ride of this distance. Give him a day or two off to recover, on light rations and, when you feel he is ready, return to your normal routine. If you both coped easily with the whole affair and feel ready to go on to a 30-miler, then do so – the procedure will be exactly the same.

When you are ready to move up to rides of 40 miles and more, the procedures change slightly, as outlined in the next chapter.

10

Longer Rides and Races

At shorter distances, most horses and riders are easily able to cope without much extra preparation or special equipment. However, once over 40 miles, your preparation and competition takes on a whole new aspect. Rides of over 40 miles become more demanding to your horse and are considered to be the start of real endurance work. Although set-speed, non-race rides cover distances up to 60 miles in a day or 100 in two, riding these is not a question of riding your set-speed 30 twice, as the demands on your horse are literally doubled. There are a few 40-mile races, but primarily racing starts at 50 miles, and the extra speed and vet-gate management means learning a new set of ropes altogether.

Rules and registrations

Before you think about attempting longer rides, you will have to read the rules of the society with which you are competing. The BHS Endurance Riding Group requires that riders and horses progress through a series of qualifications: compulsorily a 20, 30, two 40s and a 50 all at set speeds, with an optional Gold Stirrup 60-miler. To complete the qualifications, which are likely to take a couple of seasons, your horse must have a log book. For all except 20-milers, you must be a member of the ERG and your horse must be registered to compete. The SERC has a similar qualification system.

The Endurance Horse and Pony Society does not require any qualifications, membership or registrations, so that in theory a complete novice could enter a 50-mile race. However, membership entitles you to discounted entry fees and registration for trophy points for your horse. Classes are provided for novice, junior and open horses, and the society relies on riders to bring their horses on slowly through the stages. The ILDRA as yet is still in the process of formulating a system and have few competitive rides of over 40 miles. Some qualifications are interchangeable between societies, so check with the relevant secretary before you enter.

Coping with the increased mileage

The key to successfully completing more mileage is to take it slowly. Always remember that is it not distance which kills, but speed. For example, if you feel that your horse is ready to progress over 40 miles, attempt a 50-miler and aim to complete at just over the minimum speed, which will usually be 7 or 7.5mph. If you ride at 8mph you will allow yourself plenty of leeway for gates, road crossings, crewing and to come in slowly.

In set-speed rides, which currently cover up to 60 miles in a day or 100 in two, the basic procedures are always the same: vetting before and after the ride by half an hour, and a vetting at half way, which may be included in your riding time. Both you and your horse need to have a correspondingly higher level of fitness, which you may well have built up as your riding distances have gradually increased. You may find it difficult to manage with just one crew as your horse will need frequent feeding, watering and cooling out in order to complete the distance. You will find yourself in greater need of spares such as girths and numnahs; and whereas at lower distances specialist tack and equipment was not an issue, for comfort's sake, it will become one now.

Choice of venue

You will almost certainly need to stable at the ride venue for anything over 40 miles, unless you live within a stone's throw. Apart from limitations on time, it is unfair to travel a tired horse and unwise in terms of safety. Ride venues may insist that horses entered in certain classes stable at least the night after, if not also the night before a ride.

Unless you have supreme confidence in your own and your horse's fitness, it is as well to choose a venue where the route and terrain are not too demanding for each increase in mileage you make. The procedure for entry will depend largely upon the facilities available at the ride venue, which vary. If the ride is held from a racecourse, your entry and stable booking will be included together; remember that you may have to fill out a separate stable booking form. However, plenty of venues provide a list of suitable stabling nearby and it is up to you to book a stable for the relevant nights and make all the necessary arrangements with the stable owner.

Stabling away

If you are stabling, it is advisable to take your own mucking-out tools rather than relying on being able to borrow someone else's at the appropriate time. Remember that you will need to pack greater quantities of hay and feed, and the necessary buckets. Racecourse stables will also require that your horse has an up-to-date vaccination certificate in accordance with BHS rules, so if you are in any doubt, check with your vet or the ride organiser before you enter that yours is current.

If your horse is a stallion, you may need to notify the secretary on the stabling request form. If he is a weaver or has any other vices, you will need to provide for these yourself. A makeshift anti-weave device can be made with a brick on a piece of string hung from the door lintel, so take a hammer and anything else you may need. It is also advisable to take a bucket of water from home in case your horse is slow to drink 'strange' water. Horses are often affected by nerves when initially travelling to unfamiliar places and having their routines upset. Anything that you can do to minimise that upset is beneficial – remember at all times that your horse needs to stay as relaxed and calm as possible in order to do his job.

Corralling

One way that horses tend to stay more relaxed at a ride venue or overnight stay is in a corral. In effect this is a small pen or paddock on the venue field, where he has the freedom to eat grass and move freely, which is obviously beneficial after work. Corralling is increasingly an option and, provided the weather is fair and your horse can be trusted to settle, it provides a far more relaxing form of stopover for him. Corrals may be provided or you may need to take your own stakes and tape; whether you electrify it or not is your own choice, but remember that the safety of others is as important as that of your own horse. You will need to provide him with a water supply and skip out his droppings. If you are going to corral, you will need to allow space for carrying that equipment too, and time to set it up on your arrival.

At the venue: arrival

When you arrive at the venue, your priority is to have your vaccination certificates checked, if this is on the agenda. Leave someone with your vehicle while you go to the secretary to have this done and check up on your stabling or corral allocation, declare for starting the ride and collect your number. Make a note now of the time of any briefing, which will usually be the evening before the ride, as you need to be ready to attend.

If this is an overnight stay before a ride, it makes sense to unload your horse and leave him with one of your crew to graze and walk gently. This leaves the rest of you free to unload your stabling equipment and make everything ready for the horse's stay, or put up the corral. It's no fun for your horse if he is unloaded after a long journey and put straight into a bare stable, with no opportunity to stretch his legs and with no hay or water awaiting his arrival. Once your stable is ready, settle the horse in, remove his travelling gear and leave him to become accustomed to his surroundings while you sort out your own accommodation.

Rider accommodation

Again depending on the venue, this may be accommodation in bunks in the jockey's quarters of a racecourse, camping on site, or staying at a nearby bed and breakfast. The most common and easiest way is to camp on site, sleeping in a tent or in your lorry or trailer. It is worth sorting this out while it's still light, as the worst time to try and put a tent up or organise your sleeping quarters is in a small space in the dark by torch light! If you take a trailer or lorry that is going to stay put for the duration of the ride, this can safely form part of your corral and you will be near enough to hear and deal with any problems or difficulties with your horse. Always remember when parking or setting up corrals that there are plenty of other people who will want to do the same thing and you should arrange yourself considerately.

Ride briefing at an international ride: a friendly, happy atmosphere – but oh, those pre-ride nerves!

Basic procedure

The next priority is to exercise your horse, either by gently lungeing or by riding the first and last part of the route so that you know where they are for the ride. This will help to relax both of you and give you the opportunity to get used to your surroundings. Your horse needs to have some form of exercise just as he normally would the day before a ride, so

Trail-bike riders are an integral part of race riding. They mark the route, re-mark and check it during the day, and will often lead a mass start to set the pace. Like many of those involved in the sport, they are volunteers, generous people who give up their time for free, and without whom endurance rides would never take place.

that you can feed him a reasonable amount and not have to decrease his ration drastically the day before he works hard.

Briefing

If this is a set-speed ride, there is unlikely to be a briefing but there will probably be festivities of some kind, such as a barbecue or party. If it is a race ride, there will be a briefing the evening before the ride to give you information about the course and how it rides, along with difficult patches or hazards, suggested crewing points, and any alterations to the route. Take a member of your crew and your route map, and make notes on anything that you may need to recall later. It is worth checking your horse last thing that night and again, be aware that racecourse stables may close at 10pm to allow the horses a quiet period before the bustle begins the following morning.

Ride morning

For a set-speed ride, the procedure will be much as usual. You will probably be vetted on the ride morning. Start gently, meet your crew as frequently as possible, aim to complete just over the minimum speed limit and remember to keep re-fuelling, watering and cooling your horse the whole way round.

Race riding, however, is a different matter. You will probably be vetted the day before the race and, if it is a big class, this may involve two or three different vets. You may have metabolic parameters, lumps and bumps done in the stable and then be asked to trot up outside, or be vetted as a group, one after the other. On the morning of the ride you will need to be ready with your tack on about half an hour before the start, when your number will be called and you will be asked to trot up again before warming up and starting. Don't forget to report to the farrier or tack inspector if you need to.

The start of the race

Allow 15 or 20 minutes for warming up, steadily and at each pace to warm each set of muscles through. Remember to set your watch for just before 12 as the countdown begins. This period before a race is charged with atmosphere and your first mass start can be electrifying. The aim with your first race should be to take it slowly and show your horse the ropes, rather than becoming involved in the tussle. If you are doubtful about your horse's behaviour in a mass start, fit his tail with a red ribbon and, if you are doubtful about your ability to cope, let the other riders go first and start a minute or so later. You will usually be led behind a vehicle of some kind, such as a four-wheel drive wagon or a trail bike which will set the pace and show you the route for the first couple of miles. If you are starting in the dark, the vehicle provides light, and is a safety measure to keep the initial pace down, particularly if there is a stretch of roadwork.

On the trail

Once you are riding, the majority of your nerves will be dispelled, and you will be able to get on with the job of concentrating on your horse and your riding. You will have been told at the briefing how many vet gates you will have and what the procedure is for the gates themselves. On a 40- or 50-mile race ride you may only have one gate at the half-way stage, but there may well be a second gate about 5 miles from the finish. At 60 miles there will be three vet gates, and so on. The maximum is usually five during a 100-miler with other spot checks or observations along the way. The whole point of a vet gate is to pull out the horses who are in stress before it becomes a major problem.

On your first race, you should ride or walk into each gate slowly to allow your horse's heart rate to come down. Your riding speed for each leg will have to allow for time spent presenting to the vet – remember that your time on the clock will not stop until you successfully present to the vet.

Race rules

Basically the differences between a race and a longer distance set-speed ride are the speed at which you will be travelling and the limited presentation time to the vet. Your preparation, management and riding therefore has to be of a correspondingly high standard. The minimum speed for races at present is 6-6.5mph but in reality they are often ridden at double this speed. No crewing is allowed within 2km (1.2 miles) of a vet gate and you may also not stop in this distance. You must therefore be able to present to the vet within 30 minutes of arriving at a gate and pass, or, if you fail, present once again within that same 30 minutes or fail. At the final vet gate, the horse may only be presented once. Once you are seriously racing, you will be attempting to ride as fast as possible against the other competitors, present more quickly to the vet than they do and make up enough of a margin for a comfortable win – or risk a racing finish!

Race training

Once you have completed a couple of races at slow speeds and worked out your own most effective procedures and how to cope, you will want to start racing against the other competitors. In order to sustain higher speeds during competition, your preparation needs to be done accordingly at home. This will involve a higher level of training such as interval training, or incorporating some long, steady canter work at home to condition your horse to working at a higher speed for greater periods of time. Remember that speed is damaging to your horse and therefore the number of competitions you attend is likely to be limited once you reach this level, or they should be well interspersed with shorter distance or slower rides.

Lungeing at a steady canter on as wide a loop as possible is beneficial, as is as much hillwork as possible to prepare your horse's heart and lungs for the work to come. You may also find that your own personal preparation needs to move up a level, with more running at home and in training to enable you to cope and to make life easier for your horse.

Strategy

Once you start racing seriously, you will need to decide on a strategy that best suits your horse and your style of riding if you want to go for a win or placing. Firstly, don't be put off if your horse appears to cruise round everything at a solid speed without ever moving up a gear. Races can be won by sheer dint of staying power, when all around are going lame or being vetted out on pulse. Some horses, though, tend to get faster as they get older, and once they work out what it's all about.

The first leg of most races is notoriously ridden fast. Many successful race riders use the first leg as an opportunity to burn off the opposition, by riding very fast for the first section and gaining time on horses less able to cope with the speed. You have to decide if you and your horse are confident front runners and if your horse realistically has the maturity, speed and stamina to lead. Many horses go off flat out and are then too tired to maintain a rhythm, having used up their energy in an initial burst.

The second strategy is to stick with the leading pack all the way and take the opportunity to gain time at vet gates or over good going; effectively you will be racing all the way and may well end up neck and neck the last few miles into the finish, which can be exhilarating, hair-raising and risky.

Riding your own ride

The third strategy is to ride your own ride – sticking at the front of the second pack, say, and working through at a constant speed. You will pass a few flaggers on the way, moving through the pack as others burn out or are spun, and pushing on for a placing within the top five or ten as you gain ground. This is the least safe strategy in terms of winning, but will most likely result in your finishing with a horse full of running, and it still allows a chance of making up time where others tire. You will learn your own horse's plus and minus points: he may be fast uphill but slow down it; he may be fast downhill but slow on the flat; he may be fast on the flat but hate hills or roads. Either way, you will learn to make use of your own horse's strengths and weaknesses and apply those to a racing situation to your best advantage. Always remember that no matter how much adrenalin is pumping, you still need your horse intact at the end of the day if all your good work is not to go to waste.

The big 100

A one-day 100-miler is the goal that many riders are aiming for and, although these rides are always run as races, you are unlikely to attempt to race over your first-ever 100. The aim of the exercise is to get round sound and, if you have successfully completed an 80, there is no time like the present to attempt the extra 20 miles and see if you are both capable of the extra demands. It is said that there are 50-mile horses and 100-mile horses – those that perform well over shorter distances even on consecutive days but are less consistent over 100 miles in 24 hours, and those that relish the extra distance but are not fast enough or relaxed enough to settle over the shorter mileage. The only way to find out what your horse's speciality is, is to try him out!

A 100-miler will most likely start in the dark and you therefore need a light on your hat or light sticks elsewhere on your body to ensure that you don't make a mistake over rough going early on in the ride. You are also likely to need two crew vehicles leapfrogging each other, if this is permitted by the organising society. Whatever ride you choose, there will be riders racing as well as those just aiming to complete, so tuck yourself in the middle of the pack and stay out of the hunt. If it is possible, ride with a similarly paced, more experienced rider who is just out for the ride, and learn from their strategy and vet-gate presentation. Above all, remember to enjoy it – this is meant to be fun!

Vet-gate presentation

During the ride, you need to know your horse's recovery rates well enough to manage him effectively around a vet gate and, ideally, enter one ready to present. The elimination pulse rate is 64bpm both before and after trotting, and many riders will wait until a safe beat of 60bpm before asking to present. In the fit horse who is not tired, the rate will continue to drop as it is taken, and a gentle trot is unlikely to put it up more than a couple of beats. If you are racing and don't want to risk losing any time, presenting on 60bpm or 62bpm is a fairly safe bet, but you must know exactly how fresh or fatigued your horse is. If in doubt and you don't want to risk re-presentation, it is safer to wait another minute or 30 seconds and present on 58bpm rather than on 62bpm. Of course, at times like these, a pulse monitor is a big plus!

Tension is evident as the pulse rate is taken at the end of a tough ride. Spectators now attend many of the major endurance rides and riders' and crews' conduct has to be professional.

Hold time

Once through the vet, you must use your hold time wisely to give your horse the best possible chance of refuelling for the next section. Ideally the rider should be able to sit and rest and eat and drink, while the crew takes care of the horse. In practice, the rider will generally need to help and to supervise the crew's management of the horse as he may be in the best position to manage the horse sensitively from moment to moment, for optimum refuelling and relaxation.

Your management of the horse will depend largely on the weather, but is likely to centre around keeping the horse's large muscle groups warm whilst cooling him down and refreshing him so that he is in the best shape possible for the next stretch of the ride. He should be encouraged to drink as much fresh water and electrolytes as possible and given any feed which will tempt him to refuel, as well as a choice of grass and long fibre. Sugar-beet tea and carbohydrate boosts are quick energy replacers, and as much fresh fruit and vegetables (e.g. carrots, apples, swedes, turnips) as possible will help to maintain his gut function.

Gentle but active recuperation in the form of walking and grazing will help to disperse lactic acid within the muscles, whilst simply parking will

Knowing when to present to the vet is a skill, and is learned with experience. Once through the vet, keep your horse moving gently between eating and drinking to prevent him becoming stiff.

result in the horse becoming stiff and shivering. If you are in any doubt over your horse's condition, his temperature will provide a guide. A hot horse's metabolism will be working at a faster rate, therefore to get his parameters down he needs to be cool and relaxed. This is also the time to change any tack, to wash down and make your horse as comfortable as possible so that he will embark on the next stretch feeling relaxed and refreshed. During a very long hold, he needs to be kept moving gently and freely to allow his muscles to stretch, recuperate and relax as well as staying warm to be limbered up ready for the next stretch of the journey. Encourage him to stale, and do all you can to keep him quiet.

Motivation

Long holds can be detrimental to both horse and rider in terms of mental attitude. It is important that both of you stay motivated and maintain a positive attitude to the task in hand as well as to working together to complete the distance. You need to learn to fall into a rhythm together and you must help your horse throughout the distance, whether that means pacing him, letting him get on with it, or getting off and running beside him over difficult terrain. If he is tiring and slowing down, give him a breather instead of pushing him; if he gets a second wind let him go on instead of holding him back.

Whilst it is up to you to pilot him round the course safely and easily, you must also remember that he is not a machine and will work in accordance with his natural rhythm, which you must do your utmost to utilise rather than disrupt. He may need to be given confidence and motivated at various points during the ride, and you are the only one to do that; where your motivation comes from is a different case entirely, as it is likely to be from your crew! It is important at all times to maintain a positive mental outlook, which at times can be difficult given seemingly endless miles ahead. Keep the emphasis on enjoyment, relaxation and working with your horse to cover each mile at a time. Make the whole experience a pleasant one, and you will be most of the way there.

Learning from others

Riding with another, similarly paced horse can provide both you and your horse with the necessary motivation to get round, particularly if the companion is more experienced. A favourite way for first-time 100-milers to complete is in the company of an older horse who will set a sensible pace, with a rider who knows when to slow down and speed up, how to present to a vet and when to take a breather. This can be an invaluable experience for both of you in terms of learning to pace yourselves to cover the distance and finding out how your horse prefers to travel, whether from the front, the back, or in company. Some horses consistently start out fast and tire easily until they learn to conserve energy. Some start out fast but then settle into a relaxed, even, ground-covering and energy-conserving pace. Some become bored and need the company of others to tow them along, and others start out steadily but become more settled and stronger the further they go. Riding with another horse can be the key to teaching your horse that, as he has a long way to go, he'd better pace himself and conserve his energy!

However, if you don't have the luxury of teaming up with a nursemaid for the duration, just ride your own ride and aim to complete rather than race at your first attempt at the longer distance. Even when you are in with a chance, remember to listen to your horse and do your utmost to save his energy. It is vital that you only allow yourself to be towed if you need that tow, rather than setting out fast in the initial two-hour panic at the start of a race and consistently slowing up as your horse becomes tired. However, if you are in sight of the finish, using others as a final tow can be the ideal way of sparking up an uninterested horse and pulling him home!

The racing finish

It is only worth considering racing over this distance once you are confident that your horse can handle the increased speeds. You need to be a good horse manager to ride to a strategy – knowing whether to race into a vet gate, if your pulse will come down fast enough and there is plenty left in the tank, or trot in gently behind but present first; whether to race for the line after a long and arduous ride in the fight for a place, or to graciously accede. A racing finish is only worth the gamble if you are certain that your horse still has plenty of energy left and that you won't be eliminated on pulse. Sometimes the temptation is just too great anyway, for both horse and rider! Horses very rarely need training to sprint a finish when they need to, as the atmosphere and adrenalin will provide as much excitement for them as for you! However, if your horse is tired or sluggish initially, a few canters through a race course at the finish of a ride will provide all the incentive he needs.

Lameness during a racing finish can and does occur through tweaking or overworking already tired muscles. It is down to you as a rider to know whether or not your horse is capable of a final sprint and, if he is, of staying in control of his enthusiasm. The worst danger, however, is with a racing pulse. Once dismounted, if your horse's pulse is beating twice a second or more, you have serious work to do before risking presentation to the vet.

This is probably the most difficult time, and weather conditions on the day will determine how you manage your horse. Initially he should be kept gently moving and, as he is likely to be hot, you will need one person walking him to eliminate the risk of cramp while someone each

Finishing speed: a well-balanced horse and rider finishing in good condition, a sure sign of a well-managed and carefully ridden horse.

side pours on water and scrapes it off. His quarters are likely to need covering to prevent the risk of cooling down too quickly and shivering, putting the pulse rate up. If he is very hot, the water will come off warm, and you need plenty of supplies of fresh, cool water – not cold water – to keep a flow moving over his large veins all the time, cooling the blood. Keep taking the pulse, as he may reach the point where walking is keeping his heart rate up and he needs parking and massaging to keep him loose while he is cooled out. Allow him to drink as much as possible, but don't let him eat a morsel as this will also push his pulse up, risking elimination.

Elimination and pulling out

If, after all your efforts or at any time during the ride, you are spun, this can become extremely difficult to cope with mentally. This is the time when many riders blame themselves. This can be valid in order to learn from mistakes, but a lot of the time lameness is purely the result of bad luck, such as treading on a stone or twisting on a piece of rough going. Of course it is disheartening, particularly if the elimination is for an injury that requires time out of competition. However, if the vet pulls your horse out at any time during the ride, it is because this is best for your horse at that time, and therefore you should be grateful that the vet has spotted the trouble in time.

One of the most important lessons to learn in ride management is when to retire your horse. Mares in season, tired horses, young and inexperienced horses and those having an off-day, are pulled out by their riders to save the horse and because there is no point in continuing. This course of action is always worthwhile, even if there is nothing apparently wrong, as off-days can signal physical problems such as deficiencies or viral infections.

Racing protocol

Always remember that when you are racing you are one of a very few people at that ride who is travelling at a high speed and that the rest of the entries are there to gain experience, just as you once did, educating young horses and learning the ropes. The most intimidating thing for a novice is to be mown down by a race rider whose brakes have failed, or who is panicking and trying to make up time. Always slow down and warn others that you are going to pass, and overtake in a safe place. Always wait until you are past to speed up. If someone is coming up fast behind you and obviously wants to get past, move out of their way, and don't expect them to be responsible for controlling your horse if you can't. Don't ride flat out past riders whose horses are drinking or eating, even if you are racing against them. At road crossings and checkpoints, obey the stewards or marshals. Take it in turns to dismount at a gate to open and close it and don't go flying off without making sure that everyone else is safe. There are plenty of juniors racing now and the

The vet's decision is final: though it may feel miserable at the time, always take the vet's advice as it is the best possible option for your horse. Here, a panel of vets deliberate.

Pat Fowler, 1995 European Individual bronze medallist, checking Sheraton's pulse before presenting to the vet.

unaccompanied riding age limit is getting lower, so be considerate towards younger riders too. It is always worth stopping to help a rider who has problems or suffers a fall, as you never know when this might be you.

Multi-day rides

Multi-day rides are now becoming increasingly popular and the mileages are being raised. Bringing a horse out sound for a multi-day ride is entirely different to staying over 100 miles in one day, and here again you will need to be honest about your own horse's strengths and weaknesses. Some horses settle better on the second day and return lower pulse rates the further they travel; others become bored and apathetic at the idea of going out again, having done it all once already. Some horses thrive on the distance and the adrenalin of a 100 miles in a day but would balk if asked to come out again tomorrow, whilst others switch off at around 60 miles and are only enthusiastic or fast over short distances.

Next-day management

Either way, if you are aiming to bring a horse out for more than one day, your overnight management needs to be geared towards presenting a horse in top condition the day after he has competed. He will need intensive work after the first day, including a warm wash down all over to rid his coat of any sweat and scurf. His heels may need anti-bacterial treatment to prevent cracking and his large muscle groups will benefit from a good rub-down.

It can be beneficial to bandage his legs overnight if he is stabled to prevent the risk of swelling, as well as rubbing them with a cooling preparation or cold hosing. He will need access to plenty of water and electrolytes overnight, masses of long fibre such as hay or alfalfa, a couple of good feeds, and perhaps a carbohydrate boost to aid recovery.

The next morning you may need to start work early and get him out and walking in hand to limber up, as well as massaging to release tension and increase circulation all over. Rubbing down with any kind of refreshing or invigorating liniment can help to stimulate circulation and recovery, but without doubt the best remedy is some good old 'Dr Green' and gentle walking in hand.

That coveted Best Condition award

Most races will make a Best Condition award for the horse which the vets consider to be most capable of continuing. This may be awarded on lowest pulse rate at the end of the ride, but at bigger races there will be a judging, often the following day. In order to present for the Best Condition award your horse must be sparkling clean, moving loosely and freely and looking perky. The most relaxed characters are the ones who are most likely to make the grade, as their energy has not been wasted by worrying and panicking unnecessarily. The judging will usually take the form of a panel of vets looking over the horse for knocks, lumps and bumps, and a trotting out.

Preparation for judging begins as soon as the race has finished by bandaging your horse overnight to produce a set of hard, clean legs as well as using ice and witch hazel to take out any heat and swelling. Washing your horse down thoroughly with warm water and a body wash directly after the final vetting will get rid of any clots of sweat and muck and make the horse feel more comfortable. In the morning, start early by feeding him and taking him out for a gentle stroll to stretch his legs. Massaging and the use of Tellington-Jones TTeam techniques will help to loosen any stiff muscles and help to relax a tense horse. He should be plaited up and in a clean bridle. If he looks tired or stiff, don't bother taking him, as you can rest assured that there are plenty of horses who will not!

If he has pulled out lame, or is stiff or shattered the next day, your pre-ride preparation leaves something to be desired and he needs to be fitter or better managed next time. Injuries that may have been sustained late in the ride and staved off by adrenalin may show up following an overnight rest and in the following chapter, we will examine what can go wrong during a ride and how to cope with injuries.

11

Prevention and Treatment of Injury

Endurance horses are some of the best cared for equines in competitive work, purely because of the amount of veterinary attention that they receive throughout a ride. However, because endurance riding by its very nature is demanding, the sport can have a high attrition rate. Horses do sustain injuries during competition, either through bad riding or sheer bad luck. Preparation and careful management can go a long way towards preventing problems from occurring and, in effect, can prolong the working life of an endurance horse.

Avoiding injury

It is a rare horse who suffers no setback or injury during his competitive career. However, a listening, considerate rider who is aware of the horse's normal behaviour is sooner able to detect abnormalities, preventing them from becoming a major problem. As you handle your horse on a daily basis and ride him during training and in competition, you should be in the habit of noticing any changes to his action, outlook, behaviour or way of going. A slight 'ouch' over a sharp stone may cause two or three lame steps and be forgotten for the time being, but may result in bruising and uneven foot placement later in the ride or once the adrenalin has died down. A slide or twist may seem insignificant at the time, but if you continue to ride a horse who is attempting to compensate for a twinge, he will undoubtedly be lame before long. Because of this, if you are in any doubt, get off and feel for heat or walk for a while.

Fatigue should always be obvious to the considerate rider who knows his horse. A horse who is becoming tired may start to stumble slightly and lose the rhythm of his stride, lose interest and be slow to respond to you. To save him from further problems or from becoming truly fatigued, you need to pull up and take a breather or retire. A horse in trouble will give all sorts of signals as to his well-being and, as he can't talk, it is up to you to detect the problem and act upon it. Tired horses who are unable to concentrate are likely to cause themselves further trouble by pulling or tweaking muscles and tendons, which are unable to continue to work effectively. You also need to know the difference between fatigue and boredom, as some horses who don't actually like the job will completely switch off and can just as effectively end up causing themselves an injury.

Common causes of elimination

A crew member massaging the muscles of the hindquarters while the horse refuels during a vet hold. Careful massage helps to keep the blood flowing and prevents the muscles from stiffening.

Being spun during or after a ride can be a miserable experience, particularly after finishing a long or difficult ride. The most common causes of elimination are lameness and high pulse rate, depending on the weather and prevailing conditions. For example, a ride over flat terrain in hot weather will inevitably produce a higher set of pulse rates than if it were in cooler weather, and a hilly ride will produce higher pulse rates than a flat ride, particularly if riders complete at similar speeds. Over flat going, the temptation is always to go too fast, which results in a greater number of eliminations on pulse initially; where riders have slowed down because their horses have got tired, eliminations later in the ride are more likely to be for lameness. Whatever the cause of your elimination, it is important to follow the ride vet's advice from the outset and to learn

from any mistakes that you might have made. If the problem is down to you, it is also down to you to do your utmost to prevent it from happening again. If it is down to bad luck, be philosophical about it and remember that there's always another day.

Foot lameness

Almost any kind of lameness can occur during or after a ride but the most common are stone bruises over flinty going, or sole punctures. Bruises are obviously not a long-term problem in themselves and can be treated by resting until the tenderness is gone and then trimming out by your farrier. If bruising is a recurrent problem, it is advisable to take action to prevent it by fitting pads when riding over stony terrain. Many horses have soft or thin soles which cannot stand up to riding over flinty areas and this obviously limits the rides at which you can compete.

Punctures of the sole by a sharp object are also unlucky and can happen to anyone. The effects, depending on the depth and severity of penetration, can vary from nothing more than a slight nick in the horn of the sole, which can be simply cut out, to a deeper wound which, if untreated, can result in pus in the foot, developing into a major problem requiring complex veterinary attention. The majority are minor punctures due to treading on a nail or sharp stone. If in any doubt whatsoever, always consult your own vet and farrier who will be able to cut away the sole or in severe cases X-ray to ascertain the extent of the damage. Consistent foot lameness with no evident bruising can signal corns or the onset of navicular and should be investigated.

Limb lameness

The types of limb lameness which most commonly occur during a ride are muscle pulls or strains due to fatigue, a slip or fall, and pulled or strained tendons and ligaments from bad going, falling or a slide. Fatigue can affect single muscles or groups of muscles in the case of bad riding or lack of fitness. Pulled muscles require rest in order to make a full recovery but in the long term do not pose a problem. Where individual muscle tension is a problem the use of massage and Tellington-Jones TTeam techniques can help to relax the fibres and encourage circulation, aiding recovery and proper use of the limb by the horse. After a ride and before presenting to the vet, you will often see riders massaging the large muscle groups of the hindquarters to aid relaxation. Whilst these techniques can be beneficial where there is damage, veterinary advice must be sought prior to any manipulation or pressure being applied.

Tendon and ligament damage, however, will require not only a period of rest with support and cold treatments but scanning to ascertain the

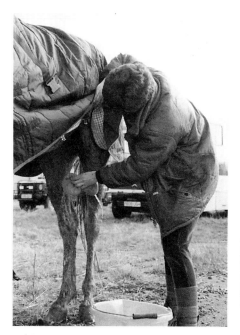

Crews should keep an eye out for cuts, grazes, lumps and bumps while preparing the horse for the vet.

A pair of ice-boots, used to help cool the legs and minimise the risk of bruising and swelling. This type of equipment is also useful for therapy on some types of injury.

degree of recovery. The damage may not cause a vast degree of lameness and, because of this, requires extremely careful management with a slow and gentle return to work. Although it is impossible at the time of injury to tell exactly what has caused the problem, it has been suggested that limb stress through overwork can cause a gradual deterioration and weakening of the structures within the leg, resulting in breakdown during work or even out in the field.

Alternatively, a twist on bad going, a fall or over-extension due to a slide can unluckily cause severe and irreparable damage. Work has been done in tendon and ligament repair using proprietary drugs, but these are costly and, of course, come without a guarantee as to their effectiveness. If the damage has been extensive, it is unlikely to hold up to endurance work in the future and can effectively finish a horse's competitive career. Some horses do return to competition but may need a year or two out of work before being gently eased back into endurance riding.

High pulse rates

Elimination on pulse rate is as common as lameness and can be down to all kinds of factors, from simple things such as excitement to the onset of dehydration and fatigue. If you are eliminated on pulse, it is important to monitor it regularly until it comes down again to a normal resting pulse, which can take several hours in a really tired or distressed animal. A high pulse may also indicate pain or stress.

Fatigue

Occasionally riders are asked or advised by the vet to withdraw from a ride as the horse is becoming fatigued. The symptoms will include depression, refusal to drink or eat, and can encompass dehydration as well as erratic metabolic parameters. It is down to the rider to be aware when the horse is tiring and, if he seems unable to recover or regain an interest in his work, to pull him from the competition without needing to be told by the vet.

Dehydration

This is a common problem in endurance riding although I have never seen a horse eliminated for it. Initial signals are a slow pinch test and persistently high metabolic rates. It may be necessary to put a saline drip into the horse if dehydration has become severe.

Synchronous Diaphragmatic Flutter (or thumps)

There are a few cases of thumps every year in competition. The symptoms will be a double thump in the diaphragm as the horse inhales, similar to a constant hiccuping motion. The causes are multi-factorial and include combined lack of electrolytes and fatigue. Thumps is more common in mares and generally occurs after 40 miles. Veterinary treatment usually takes the form of administering electrolytes and fluid.

Colic

Colic can occur during or post-ride as a result of dehydration, stress, or injudicious feeding and watering during a ride. Depending on the severity, symptoms will include sweating, stomach cramps and pain, high pulse rate and temperature, and behavioural abnormalities such as attempting to lie down or kick at the stomach. Treatment will depend on symptoms displayed but may include administering fluids or liquid paraffin.

Azoturia

This has been discussed in depth in the chapter on feeding and requires a change in management at home prior to competition.

Long-term problems

With the cumulative mileage involved in endurance training and competition, other physical problems are not inevitable but are common. Over-riding and concussion are seen as the two major contributory factors of problems such as navicular syndrome, concussion laminitis, degenerative joint disease and arthritic conditions. Although specific causes of each of these conditions are ill-defined, and they can occur in horses from all walks of life, each is thought to be aggravated and exacerbated by continuous hard work or by short-term excessive concussion. Therefore anything that you can do to minimise the effects of concussion to your horse during work can only be beneficial.

Injury management

If your horse has been eliminated due to injury or another physical problem requiring rest, his treatment at home in recovery will be down to you. He may just require time off from work, to be turned out to relax, have his feed cut right down and a break from the stresses of constant training and competition. However, some injuries require that the horse be box-rested for a period of time following the initial injury and, where a very fit horse is concerned, this can be a recipe for disaster if not carefully managed. As his feed will need to be cut right back and exercise is out of the question, the primary problems will be caused by a hungry horse who wants to go out and tear around but is not even given the opportunity to leave the box. Vices can develop under such circumstances and temperament can become a problem.

The priority is to keep your horse as occupied as possible. Even with a laid-back character, boredom and tension can become a problem for any horse who is box-rested 24 hours a day. Changing to a small-holed haynet will mean that he has to take longer to eat his hay and, if he is on straw, changing to shavings will prevent him from continually devouring his bed. Leaving a radio playing nearby (under cover) can provide comfort, particularly if left tuned to a channel where the majority of the broadcast is made up of speaking and commentary rather than music. Providing fresh branches of an edible tree such as ash will provide an entertaining and natural diversion as well as a change of snack. Having a pet, such as a rabbit in the box or a friendly stable cat, provides company and interest.

If he refuses to settle in the stable but becomes frustrated and is likely to cause himself further injury, corralling him in the corner of his regular paddock, in sight of his friends, can provide a means to confine him in a smaller space. In this way he can't come to much mischief but won't feel completely isolated. It is important during this time to continue to spend as much time as possible in your horse's company, other than just changing bandages or carrying out therapeutic treatments, as he will quickly become sick of the sight of you if all you do is fiddle with the painful bits. Grooming him will form a major part of the daily routine, to provide attention, interest and to help to retain muscle tone, which will slacken off due to the lack of work.

Veterinary treatment

Where any competition horse is concerned, it is of fundamental importance that you have access to a knowledgeable, sympathetic and preferably reputable horse vet at home. Following problems in competition you need an expert who will diagnose, treat and hopefully speed your horse's return to work. Many vets are now becoming increasingly aware of the demands that endurance riding places on the horse and are developing a greater respect for the training and commitment that goes into producing a horse capable of competing at longer distances. It is important to have an experienced professional on your side, as you may need to call him in to take a blood test simply because the horse seems off-colour or didn't perform particularly well during a ride.

If your own vet is not aware of regulations barring use of various drugs that may be used to treat your horse, the BHS publish a list of prohibited substances and a guide is available through Jockey Club regulations. There may be a withdrawal period following treatment of an injury, for example with anti-inflammatories, even if it was just a knock in the field at home. Though blood tests are generally only taken from selected horses at major rides, it is not worth the risk of subjecting your horse to competitive work with a substance in his system that may be masking his symptoms.

Alternative therapy

Your vet will be the first person who advises you over suitable treatment and management of your horse's injury. Depending on the injury and the extent of the damage sustained, he will also be able to give a good idea of long-term prognosis as far as the horse's future competitive career is concerned, although this can be difficult until some degree of recovery has been made. Should full recovery fail under conventional veterinary supervision, endurance riders on the whole are now looking to a wider field of expertise in improving performance and ability.

With herbal supplements, chiropractors, physiotherapists and therapeutic massage techniques forming part of the endurance rider's daily routine, an increasing variety of equine therapists and alternative treatments are being employed in healing injuries with varying degrees of success. When conventional techniques have been exhausted, it is worthwhile attempting to find a more holistic approach, i.e. a whole-animal look at well-being rather than just treating the specific problem in isolation. It is widely accepted that one injury or condition can be caused by another or can, in turn, cause another, for example in cases of muscle wastage and uneven action following injury to one leg. Problems can become self-perpetuating and unless a rounded view is taken, including teaching the horse to use himself properly again all over, a full recovery can become protracted or prove impossible.

Returning to work

Any return to work will be made under veterinary supervision and should be slow and cautious. If in any doubt over your horse's readiness to work under saddle, it can be safer to walk him out in hand first for a couple of weeks, particularly if he has been completely box-rested. Some horses, however, find it impossible to settle in hand and prefer to be ridden, even if only for 10 minutes at a walk.

Electric fencing can be used to extend his area of turnout prior to releasing him with his friends and risking a sudden helter-skelter gallop and the accompanying handbrake turns around the field.

If you feel the slightest twinge, notice any heat or are in any doubt over your horse's soundness, return to a lower level of work until you feel ready to progress again. Although veterinary advice is essential you will know your horse better than anyone, and should be well aware of his capabilities. There are today, however, other means of providing a return to work apart from just riding. Swimming facilities are less expensive than previously and provide a means of exercising the horse without bearing weight on the legs. The use of a treadmill can also be informative as well as beneficial and many horses, injured or not, will often go crooked on introduction to a treadmill, indicating uneven muscle development and usage. Both of these therapies provide an ideal means of controlled, gentle work for the horse returning to activity after a prolonged rest, and are no longer prohibitively expensive. It goes without saying that a recovering horse should never be pushed too soon, as the risk of further damage or complete breakdown can never be discounted during the recovery period.

Other considerations: the skin

This is one vital part of the horse's anatomy which is often ignored but which has a bearing on his physical and competitive well-being. The endurance horse's skin suffers more than any other horse's from problems with condition, due to the volume of sweat that it produces during a ride and in training at home. It is also constantly being washed during a ride and in training, all of which can result in sweat rash due to clogged pores being improperly washed, or sore, dry and flaky skin due to constant washing and drying out. Various products are available to help to condition the coat and skin and occasional use of these can be helpful to maintain elasticity, particularly in very thin-skinned horses. Pink skin is also more vulnerable to sunburn and may need to be protected with a total sun-block during a long or very hot ride as well as at home.

Dry, damaged, out-of-condition skin is more vulnerable to bacterial infection, and a universal problem with the endurance horse is a mud-fever type syndrome directly after and occasionally even during a long ride. This appears to particularly affect pink skin, though plenty of horses with an abundance of pink skin never apparently suffer. The problem occurs as a result of the constant damp, warm conditions in the heels allowing bacteria to flourish – this can actually cause lameness post-ride with swelling, cracking and stiffness the following day. Antibacterial washes are available from your vet in an attempt to combat the problem and all kinds of remedies are worth a try; I have found the most successful to be rubbing flowers of sulphur into the heels before, during and after a ride as well as at home for several days until the condition has cleared up. It can, however, be difficult to produce a horse with this type of problem for multi-day competition.

The mouth

Another neglected area of the endurance horse is the mouth. Endurance horses are often seen to have faulty brakes and steering, which can largely be combatted not only through schooling but also by maintenance and management at home. Many riders fail to have their horse's teeth rasped even once a year, yet keeping the teeth smooth and free from rough edges makes an enormous contribution to keeping the horse balanced and working correctly. He will be more able to accept the bit, enabling braking and steering even under emergency or racing situations. Equine dentists or dental attention from your vet is not expensive today and six-monthly check-ups can make the difference between a horse who works happily and in a balanced way and one who is unbalanced or difficult to control.

Respiration problems and allergies

Wind problems which affect the amount of oxygen that the horse can take into his lungs are serious in any competition horse, effectively restricting the pace and duration of his work. Horses with allergies and COPD do compete, but need extremely careful management at home and during a ride. Many horses are allergic to certain pollens, in particular that from rape crops, yet compete successfully under veterinary advice. Provided that the horse is kept fit and the irritants in his environment are kept to an absolute minimum, he should be able to function effectively.

Keeping a horse injury free in top-level competition, season after season, is a feat in itself. Here, Jill Thomas and the consistently successful Egyptian Khalifa prepare for vetting.

Mental stress

It is a fact that endurance horses need to love their work. It is physically impossible to push a horse who doesn't want to go, around any sort of mileage at all. Therefore, he must be fresh, enthusiastic and interested if he is to compete to the best of his ability. Constantly pounding around the same training circuits at home simply adds up to a bored horse, who is unlikely to enthuse over yet more miles in a different place. Your horse needs to be kept alert and happy at home through management of his daily routine and variation in his training schedule, to produce him in a sharp but relaxed condition, ready to tackle new and challenging terrain.

Endurance horses everywhere benefit from a couple of months' lay-off at the end of every season, to unwind, grow fat and hairy and take life easy – simply being a horse for a while. Similarly, many horses who have come new to the sport and had two or three good seasons benefit from six months out of hard work or in another discipline to maintain a fresh approach. This is an ideal opportunity for mares who are doing well to be given time out to breed for a season, being brought back into work at the end of the second season following weaning.

There is a high turnover in endurance horses who peak in fitness in their third or fourth year. Lacking the maturity and experience to work in a relaxed but ongoing manner, with enthusiastic riders on board, they tend to get faster and faster, largely as a result of speed training at home, resulting in all kinds of physical problems. Any kind of recurrent problem or string of injuries signals the warning for a lay-off, and should always be heeded.

On taking action to cut the workload in time, the horse should be let down and allowed to relax, and returned to competitions at a later date. This is preferable to risking a short, meteoric career and the almost inevitable burn-out.

Retirement

Many horses are pulled out of competition prematurely due to an injury that spells the end of that horse's career. However, plenty of tough little horses stay sound and healthy well into their later years. The decision to retire a horse completely from active competition can be a difficult one if the horse is in his late teens but fighting fit and was a late starter. In many cases, endurance horses successfully compete into their late teens and early twenties, having been brought on carefully and slowly during a long and gradual training process. It can be difficult to wind down a horse who plainly loves his work, but the process is inevitable as bones and tissues take longer to repair and regenerate following injury and structures that have had a lifetime's work become weaker and less able to withstand the load.

If your horse doesn't begin to tell you when he has had enough but you think he has, or if he is beginning to favour staying in his field for a gentle stroll and a relax rather than going out for a mad two-hour training session, it is up to you to make the decision to cut down the workload. Reducing the load is as simple a matter as your winding-up process was, involving cutting down to lower-level rides at slower speeds, and dropping back to set-speed rides rather than the flat-out rush if you have been racing. Old-timers should never be pushed, in the same way that youngsters need to take things easy. Many live out a happy retirement ambling round the block or pottering round short-distance pleasure rides if they really are workaholics and refuse to relax!

12

Giving Something Back

Once you have become an addicted endurance rider and begun to enjoy success at rides and form friendships with those whom you meet along the way, the time comes to think about giving something back to the sport. As endurance riding is an amateur sport and must necessarily remain so, it is run by a vast, unpaid workforce, many of whom have nothing to do with horses themselves but are roped in or offer to give up their time to help. Without such people, it would not be possible for rides to take place, and it is up to every rider to make sure that, in turn, he or she helps to provide some enjoyment for others.

Help is welcome in countless forms, not least of which includes offering to assist at a ride, either by vet writing, manning a checkpoint, being secretary on the day, or taking on the role of one of the many helpers who are on hand to make sure that whatever needs doing to make the day run smoothly is done. For those with more experience or with organisational skills, the offer to run or organise a ride is never refused, be it taking on an existing ride or establishing a completely new fixture.

Running a ride seems a bit like having a baby: there is a long period of gradual and increasingly anxious build-up to the big day, upon which many organisers vow never to do it again...but they almost always do! The best reason for putting on a ride is a lack of fixtures in your area, or discovering a route which you think would make an ideal competition ride. The organisers' motto is: 'Don't moan about it, run one,' and many riders who take up the challenge find that their modest initial fixture becomes a major annual event. Ride organisers' packs are available from secretaries of the various societies, and help is always forthcoming from other ride organisers, past and present.

Just as the roles of helpers and organisers of rides are vital but often thankless and largely ignored by the participating population, work on committees and regional groups is another aspect of endurance riding which tends to go unnoticed. Many hours of unpaid and unrewarded time goes into behind-the-scenes work, spent on making the societies themselves tick. Simple things like ordering rosettes, printing vet sheets and ride schedules, and registering horses for trophy points are time-consuming jobs which all have to be done by somebody. The main organising societies and their regional counterparts are crying out for people to take on roles such as helping to catalogue riders and horses, putting together newsletters, starting up regional groups, or organising educational and fund-raising seminars and evenings.

Each organising body has an annual general meeting, and committee members are needed to help to administer rule changes, new rides and help to move the sport forward. Regional groups work in the same way and carry out an enormous number of regional rides and other activities every year that serve not only to bring riders together, but also to raise funds for the central organisation. As the sport as a whole and major events in particular need sponsorship funding in order to remain affordable to competitors and viable to organisers, fund-raising is an activity which can never be ignored and is essential. Many rides are in fact run in order to raise money and, while some return a loss, the need to find new ways to bring cash into the sport is a constant priority.

Apart from enabling the sport to continue on home ground, fund-raising is an essential part of maintaining an international profile. British teams have had some resounding successes in recent years, and in order to continue to compete on a level with our counterparts internationally, a constant inflow of cash is required. Trips abroad are often self-funded and riders are required to put some personal money into competing internationally. Thus, the only way to produce teams of a level of experience and ability to compete with the best in the world is to provide the means for them to do so. In order to gain essential sponsorship, profile- and awareness-raising are always on the agenda in terms of finding new ways to publicise the sport and interest the media in our activities.

As the public rapidly becomes aware of endurance riding, the future direction of the sport is open to question more so than at any other time. As numbers of riders entering the sport increases, safety and riding protocol become more of a priority and the need for rider education remains paramount. Issues are constantly raised, such as the over-riding of young or novice horses, lack of rider training and ability, the effect of endurance riding on the countryside and so on, and need to be addressed and remedied in some way. As yet there exists no formal training programme for endurance riders wishing to progress, and although seminars and training days with limited space availability are run from time to time, these are by no means held often enough or with sufficient places to benefit the majority of endurance riders.

There is, every so often, debate over the future of endurance riding as a whole and the possibility of its attaining professional status. In order that equine welfare remains the paramount criteria, this is unlikely ever to happen. However, in order that the sport moves forward and continues to break new ground and grow in the right direction, the societies need to work together towards a mutually agreed and beneficial future, for the good of horses and riders involved in the sport in our country and worldwide. It is hoped that the next few years will see all the British societies joining together as one endurance body, as is suggested by forward thinkers, representing the interests of riders at home and abroad with one unified voice.

Useful Addresses

BHS ERG (British Horse Society
  Endurance Riding Group)
ERG Office
British Horse Society
British Equestrian Centre
Stoneleigh Park
Kenilworth
Warwickshire
CV8 2LR
01203 696697

EHPS of GB (The Endurance
  Horse and Pony Society of
  Great Britain)
Ossie Hare
Mill House
Mill Lane
Stoke Bruerne
Towcester
Northamptonshire
NN12 7SH

SERC (Scottish Endurance
  Riding Club)
Lindsay Wilson
The SERC Secretary
9 Elliot Road
Jedburgh
Roxburghshire
TD8 6HN
01835 863823

ILDRA (Irish Long Distance
  Riding Association)
Sharon Perry
188 Ballynahinch Road
Ballykeel
Dromore
Co. Down
BT25 1EU

Country and Distance Rider Magazine
Cecile Park Publishing
55-63 Goswell Road
London, EC1V 7EN
0171 490 3398

ELDRIC (European Long
  Distance Ride Conference)
M Jacques Robin
Logis de Seneuil
F-79410 Cherveux
France
+33 49 75 02 25

AERC (American Endurance
  Ride Conference)
701 High Street
Suite 203
Auburn
CA 95603
USA
+1 916 823 2260

Index

References to illustrations are in *italic*.